NORTH QUEENSLAND WET TROPICS

The north Queensland humid tropical region contains the most habitat diversity, most diverse biotic communities, and most species of higher plants in the only continuous area of its size in Australia. It is one of the most significant regional ecosystems in the world: as a key to the origins and ancient habitats of primitive flowering plants; as a key to the processes of past climatic sifting of taxa and community types; and as a biological link with the tropics to the north and with the temperate zones southwards to Tasmania and eastwards to South America.

Dr Len Webb
Rainforest Ecologist

NORTH QUEENSLAND
WET TROPICS

A GUIDE FOR TRAVELLERS

ROD RITCHIE

WITH CONTRIBUTIONS BY

PAUL CURTIS, AILA KETO
KEITH SCOTT, GARRY WERREN

PHOTOGRAPHS BY

PAUL CURTIS, C. & D. FRITH
PETER LIK, MIKE PROCIV
ROD RITCHIE, MIKE TRENERRY

RAINFOREST PUBLISHING

Published by Rainforest Publishing
PO Box 51, Millers Point, NSW 2000 AUSTRALIA

Although the author and publisher have endeavoured to ensure that the information is as accurate as possible, they accept no responsibility for any loss, injury or inconvenience sustained by any person using this book.

National Library of Australia Cataloguing-in-Publication data:
Ritchie, Rod, North Queensland Wet Tropics
Bibliography, Includes index
ISBN 0 947134 10 7
1. Rainforests – Queensland – Guidebooks
2. National parks and reserves – Queensland – Guidebooks.
I Title. (Series: World Heritage Australia)
919.430463

Design and typesetting by Rainforest Publishing
Maps by MapGraphics
Produced by Mandarin Offset
Front cover: Mossman Gorge/Dainty Tree Frogs
Photos: Peter Lik/Mike Trenerry
Back cover: Bicton Hill/Herbert River Ringtail Possum/Tchupalla Falls
Photos: Paul Curtis/C. & D. Frith/Rod Ritchie
Inside covers: Tree ferns   Photo: Peter Lik

A percentage of the proceeds from the sale of this book will go towards the
Australian Wet Tropics Rainforest Foundation
which is being established to raise funds to promote all aspects of rainforest preservation including education, scientific research, visitor infrastructure, Aboriginal cultural projects, reforestation and interpretation facilities.

For further information contact the Wet Tropics Management Authority
PO Box 2050, Cairns, Queensland 4870 AUSTRALIA   Tel 070 52 0555

FRONT COVER & PAGE 2
The lowland gorges such as Mossman Gorge in Daintree National Park are important refuge areas where plants retreated during times of adverse climate. The lowland complex mesophyll vine forest supports some very restricted species. P. LIK

LEGEND FOR MAPS

Major Highway	▬▬	Major town	●
Major Road (sealed)	▬▬	Minor town	•
Major Road (unsealed)	▬ ▬	Tourist point of interest	•
Minor Road (sealed)	▭	Ranger Station	🚻
Minor Road (unsealed)	▬ ▬	Airfield	✈
Track (4 Wheel Drive Only)	▬ ▬	Domestic Airport	✈
Walking Trail	· · · ·	International Airport	✈
Tourist Boat Route	├ ─ ┤	Campsite with facilities	⛺
Railway with station or siding	├●┤	Backpackers/Youth Hostel	🏠
River or creek	∿	Crocodile Warning	🐊
Aboriginal Land	▨	Reef activities - snorkeling, diving	🤿
Aboriginal Land in World Heritage Area	▨	Lookout or viewpoint	👀
National Park	▨	Canoeing	🛶
National Park in World Heritage Area	▨	Walking Trails	🚶
World Heritage Area	▨	Swimming	🏊
Other land	▨	Picnic tables	🪑
Urban Area	▭	Coral Reef	▭

Kilometres

0   5   10   15   20

Scale 1:600 000

Factors relating to the maps in this book change with time. The publisher would be pleased to be informed of any errors or omissions and they will be corrected in future editions.

🌐 **MAPgraphics**   All maps drawn and designed by MAPgraphics, Brisbane
© MAPgraphics, 1995

CONTENTS

ACKNOWLEDGEMENTS

A book such as this only comes about with the cooperation of many people. Thanks are due to Paul Curtis who wrote most of the walks in the Kuranda/Cairns area as well as Tully Gorge NP, Millstream Falls, Millaa Millaa Waterfall Circuit, Bellenden Ker, Goldfields Track, Ella Bay and the Kennedy Track. Paul also co-wrote the section on photography.

Within the context of this book it has only been possible to give an introduction to the region's history, so the reader who wants more should look for the recently published *Kie Daudai: Notes and Sketches from Cape York* by Edwina Toohey. Aboriginal life in the rainforest can best be learned from local people such as Hazel Douglas, whose advice was appreciated and who operates the award-winning Native Guide Safari Tours.

For pointing out some of the glaring errors I am indebted to Garry Werren who also wrote the section on Fauna and who assisted with the picture captions. Greg Armbrust provided part of the text on Hinchinbrook Island and Ros Ollermann was forthcoming with information about the Cardwell district.

The Wet Tropics Management Authority has been helpful in many ways, including allowing the section 'Why a World Heritage Area' to be reprinted and I would like to thank Peter Hitchcock, Andrew McKenzie and Mike Stott. Department of Environment and Heritage staff who read and made suggestions include Pamela Harmon-Price, Pam Bigelow, Bill French, Rupert Russell, Nicola Moore, Jenny Smith, Dave Green, Dave Flett and Pauline de Vos.

Aila Keto and Keith Scott wrote the section on Biogeography and Flora and they have long been supportive of the project and readily allowed access to Rainforest Conservation Society files.

The maps were produced by Kim Wright with professional dedication. Tricia McCallum illustrated the Walking Safely section, while Swee-Eng Chia was responsible for the copy editing. George Hirst helped with the research on Townsville and Steve Noakes provided information on visitors to Cairns. On the production side Hari Ho and Joy Willis have been helpful, while Laurie Guthridge offered design suggestions.

The photographers, Peter Lik, Clifford and Dawn Frith, Paul Curtis, Mike Prociv and Mike Trenerry have been tolerant towards my wishes. Kerrie Fitzmyers from Rainforest Habitat also supplied transparencies.

While all the people listed here, and others, have been generous with their time and have made useful suggestions, all errors and omissions remain the responsibility of the writer.

FOREWORD

AS I WRITE IT'S RAINING; THE WET SEASON HAS FINALLY ARRIVED. It may not be the best time for the tourism industry but we accept the Wet with gratitude for rain is the lifeblood of the rainforest. The trees explode with new growth, the creeks and waterfalls again become a spectacle, and we spend our nights listening to rain drumming on an iron roof and the constant chorusing of tree frogs.

Too few people experience the rainforest in the Wet. While there are obvious mobility problems with many tracks and roads impassible or closed to prevent wheels churning the mud into a quagmire, where rainforest is accessible it is a delight to visit. The colours seem more intense and often a shroud of mist provides an ethereal quality. And you will certainly appreciate how efficient the rainforest canopy is as nature's umbrella – you will hear the rain falling on the trees above and be aware of the constant dripping of leaves all around – but for the walker the rainforest floor is surprisingly dry.

Rod Ritchie's guide to Australia's Wet Tropics World Heritage Area is a guide for all seasons – both of them! The book will find a ready audience with locals looking for interesting weekends to international visitors on fast and furious timetables looking for the 'ultimate' rainforest experience.

Like much of the author's other work it is an eclectic presentation drawing on references as diverse as explorers' notebooks and scientific texts. And readers will readily appreciate that there is much more to the Wet Tropics World Heritage Area than just the Daintree and Cape Tribulation. It is part of the Wet Tropics Management Authority's policy to spread some of the visitor load away from the Daintree into other less 'popular' areas – mainly from the perspective of better managing visitor impacts but also to promote regional equity in spreading the visitor revenue across more communities.

Our World Heritage Area stretches from just north of Townsville to just south of Cooktown – from Paluma and Mt Spec in the south to Cedar Bay and Black Mountain in the north. In between are Queensland's highest mountains – Bartle Frere and Bellenden Ker; the crater lakes on the Atherton Tableland – Barrine and Eacham; spectacular waterfalls like Wallaman, Jourama and the 'waterfall circuit' at the top of Palmerston. For the driver there is the incomparable Cook Highway with its magnificent coastal scenery north of Cairns, the

Palmerston Highway west from Innisfail up through the Johnstone Gorge and for the more adventurous, unsealed roads like Kirrama Range Road which will take you from the coast just north of Cardwell up through the southern end of the Tableland. Presenting the Wet Tropics' values is part of our Primary Goal. We have an interest in ensuring that your visit to these special rainforests is not only safe and enjoyable, but you also take away a feeling and an understanding of why this is one of the top one-hundred or so natural sites on earth. Try and remember that your visit to the Wet Tropics is one of almost five million visits to Wet Tropics sites each year. Please help us to take care of this special place and please take care of yourself – most accidents in the rainforest result from personal negligence. We have one of the safest rainforests on earth and we would like to keep it that way.

This book provides the wherewithal for organising any number of high quality experiences in Australia's Wet Tropics. Rod Ritchie writes with the insight of a good guide – lots of tips and observations and enough variety to satisfy the widest recreational tastes. Please enjoy this book and what's more use it wisely to enjoy your next Wet Tropics experience.

Peter Hitchcock

Executive Director
Wet Tropics Management Authority

A NOTE TO READERS

At first glance it would appear that there is a warning for every activity in this book. There are two reasons for this. First, I am passing on the words of caution from authorities who always must be careful to cover themselves. Second, like them, I do not wish to be held responsible for anyone coming to grief through bad luck or poor judgement. However, from my experiences of walking a variety of rainforests on the east coast of Australia for many years, I have yet to suffer more than the odd leech bite or stray tick. This is because I walk with awareness, stay on the trails and have learnt to recognise the potential forest hazards. Once you are at this stage you are ready to really enjoy your walks.

There are no small-scale maps in this book, rather I have concentrated on making it easy to get to the beginning of the walks. Because the walks described here are all on well-formed paths there is little chance of getting lost. You may, however, wish to pick up the various national park and state forest brochures that often include a track map.

As well as details on the best walks within the Wet Tropics World Heritage Area, I have included a number of other places, mostly those with rainforest walking trails. While the information is not as detailed, there is enough to get you started or enthused.

REGIONAL OFFICES

Regional offices of the National Parks and Wildlife Service (known as the Queensland Department of Environment and Heritage or QDEH) and State Forests (known as Queensland Department of Primary Industry – Forest Service or QDPI-FS) have a range of brochures which complement the walks in this book and staff are available during office hours to assist with park conditions and directions. The relevant authority to contact is noted with each walk and the contact phone numbers are as follows:

QDEH, Cape Tribulation
 (070) 98 0052
QDEH, Mossman (070) 98 2188
QDEH, Cairns (070) 52 3096
QDPI-FS, Atherton (070) 91 1844
QDEH, Lake Eacham
 (070) 95 3768
QDEH, Josephine Falls
 (070) 67 6304
QDEH, Innisfail (070) 64 5115
QDPI-FS, Ingham (077) 76 2354

QDEH, Mission Beach
 (070) 68 7183
QDEH, Edmund Kennedy NP,
 (070) 66 8890
QDEH, Cardwell (070) 66 8601
QDPI-FS, Cardwell (070) 66 8804
QDEH, Ingham (077) 76 1700
QDEH, Jourama (077) 77 3112
QDEH, Paluma (077) 70 8526
QDEH, Townsville (077) 22 5292
QDEH, Magnetic Is. (077) 78 5378

CLIMATE

The best time to visit the Wet Tropics is from April to November when the weather is relatively dry and and the temperatures somewhat mild. With annual rainfalls varying from 1200 mm to 4000 mm, and up to 10,000 mm in places, the Wet Season, from December to March, can make places difficult to visit. However, if you are prepared to accept the inconvenience, rain and steamy heat, the forests have a special atmosphere at this time which is quite unique. The summer temperature on the coast averages 30° C in the Wet Season and about 20° C in the Dry Season. On the Tableland the weather is cooler and somewhat drier which makes for better summer visiting, although be prepared for the lower temperatures in winter when it can get below 10° C.

Because the weather is often variable it is best to be prepared for all conditions. The shady forest can be quite cool, particularly in the evening at higher altitudes, so pack a warm top. As well, be prepared for wet weather as rain can fall any time of the year regardless of the season. Obviously, the Wet Season is the time when many of the forest tracks become slippery and some roads may become impassible or are closed to traffic. At these times there are places without access problems and with developed pathways which are easier to visit.

PLACES WITH EASY ACCESS

Some of the places mentioned in this book are suitable for people who have difficulty in walking great distances, are unsteady on their feet or are confined to wheelchairs. Many of the day use sites have short walking tracks and others are near lookouts that are close to the carparks. Some walking trails have ramps, well-formed level tracks or boardwalks, or a combination of all three. They are:

Daintree National Park: Marrdja Boardwalk and Goolkee Track
Cairns: Crystal Cascades, Flecker Botanic Gardens
Kuranda: Barron Gorge Lookout
Atherton Tableland: Crater Lakes National Park, Malanda Falls
    Conservation Park, The Curtain Fig, The Cathedral Fig,
    Mt Hypipamee National Park and Millstream Falls
Innisfail-Tully: Boulders Wildland Park, Eubenangee Swamp National
    Park, Lacey Creek Forest Walk, Licuala State Forest, Josephine Falls
Cardwell-Ingham: Murray Falls State Forest, Broadwater State Forest
    and Edmund Kennedy National Park
Paluma Range National Park: McClelland's Track

GETTING THERE AND GETTING AROUND

International airlines flying into Cairns include Air New Zealand, Air Niugini, Cathay Pacific, Garuda Airlines, Japan Airlines and Qantas. Interstate services are offered by Ansett, Eastwest Airlines and Qantas, while regional flights are available from Flightwest, Sunstate and Cape York Air Services.

The Sunlander train departs for Cairns and places in between from Brisbane on Tuesday, Thursday and Saturday while the Queenslander departs on Sunday.

There are daily coach services to Cairns and stops in between from Brisbane and Sydney with Greyhound-Pioneer, and McCafferty's. Local bus services serve most towns on a regular basis and mostly depart from the main terminus at Trinity Wharf, Cairns. A variety of guided tours to selected sites, mostly only to places north of Cairns or the Atherton Tableland, are offered by local tour operators.

At most times of the year the places mentioned in this book can be reached by an ordinary motor vehicle. By taking your time to see a variety of places you are able to fully appreciate the diversity of the Wet Tropics. Car or campervan rentals are popular and a number of companies compete for business offering a range of vehicles. The Bruce Highway, running from Townsville to Cairns, is the main arterial for the roads to the different sites. The Captain Cook Highway is the main road north of Cairns to Mossman, while the Kennedy, Gillies and Palmerston Highways lead to Mareeba, Atherton and Ravenshoe respectively.

WET TROPICS VISITOR CENTRES

These centres provide a range of information and interactive experiences for visitors. Phone enquiries are taken by those with numbers listed here.

- Daintree Rainforest Environment Centre, 070 98 9171
- Big Croc Cafe, Daintree River Crossing
- Rainforest Habitat, Port Douglas
- Lake Morris Teahouse, Copperlode Dam
- Teahouse, Lake Barrine
- Mission Beach Environment Interpretive Centre, 070 68 7197
- Visitor Centre, Ingham, 077 76 5211
- Frosty Mango, Mutarnee (South of Ingham)
- Townsville Enterprise Centre

PLACES TO STAY

There is a large range of accommodation, particularly in and around Cairns. A complete listing is a book in itself. The places mentioned here are those which promote themselves to people looking for a rainforest experience. All are located close to the rainforests and in many cases set within them. The choices in the Daintree region are great, while in other places they are not yet so wide.

Prices given are a guide only and apply to the high season from April to January. Many places offer discount rates for other periods as well as packages for food and accommodation. Rates quoted are for twin share, per night in a standard room or unit.

Mossman/Daintree

Bloomfield	Weary Bay	$355	070 35 9166
Silky Oaks	Mossman	$350	070 98 1666
Daintree EcoTourist Lodge	Daintree	$284	070 98 6100
Ferntree Resort	Cape Tribulation	$210	070 98 0000
Coconut Beach Resort	Cape Tribulation	$180	070 98 0033
Heritage Lodge	Cape Tribulation	$129	070 98 9138
Club Daintree	Cape Kimberley	$90	070 90 7500
Lync Haven	Alexandra Bay	$65	070 98 9155
Rainforest Retreat	Daintree	$60	070 98 9101
Crocodylus Village	Cow Bay	$45	070 98 9105
PK's Jungle Village	Cape Tribulation	$44	070 98 0040

Cairns/Kuranda

Rainforest Grove	Cairns	$75	070 53 6366
Cassowary House	Kuranda	$390	070 93 7318
Kuranda Rainforest Resort	Kuranda	$120	070 93 7555
Cedar Park Rainforest Resort	Kuranda	$99	070 93 7077

Atherton Tableland

Chambers Apartments	Lake Eacham	$80	070 95 3754
Atherton Backpackers	Atherton	$28	070 91 3552
Mungalli Falls Outpost	Millaa Millaa	$40	070 97 2358
Malanda Hotel Motel	Malanda	$34	070 96 5101

Innisfail/Tully

The Point Resort	Sth. Mission Beach	$160	070 68 8154
Mission Beach Backpackers	Mission Beach	$34	070 68 8317

Cardwell/Ingham

Kookaburra Holiday Hostel	Cardwell	$35	070 66 8648

Townsville

Misthaven	Paluma	$50	077 70 8520

WALKING SAFELY IN THE RAINFOREST

The walks in this book have been chosen because they are at places which are relatively easy to get to and because they generally have the facilities to handle the number of people who choose to visit. They range in time from one hour to half-day.

The grades vary from easy to moderate for people of average fitness. There are also some longer and full-day walks which may require a higher level of fitness and there are several important things to do if you decide to undertake these:

• Let the local ranger, or at least friends, know of your intentions and details of your party before departure.
• Carry a good map and compass.
• Wear a watch.
• Carry plenty of water because there are times of the year when water can be scarce. It is best not to drink from streams.
• Carry some food.
• Be prepared for sudden and dramatic changes in weather conditions.
• Remember to wear sensible clothing, and take a hat and sunscreen for beach and open-area walks. Take something warm for upland walks and pack a light raincoat.

Compared to most activities the odds of getting seriously hurt on any of the walks in this book are slim, particularly if you stay on the recommended tracks. It is worth knowing, however, that there are plants and animals in the rainforest that you should be able to recognise because some of them are able to bite or sting. The way to avoid having to remedy a painful situation is to walk with awareness and to stop and check yourself regularly. Look out for the following:

Leeches
Related to earthworms, leeches have short muscular bodies that are divided into segments. They have a sucker at each end, and are able to stretch out and move a long way in search of their prey. They even have organs which enable them to detect light, shape and smell. When their jaw latches on with one of its suckers, the tiny cut to your skin is injected with an anaesthetic so you feel no pain. When the leech has had its fill it drops off and because it has injected an anticoagulant, your blood keeps flowing for a while.

You can deter leeches by applying insect repellent to your ankles, or by rubbing some eucalyptus oil on your lower legs above your socks. Best of all, just make the occasional inspection and intercept them on their way to a meal. They are easy to remove.

Scrub-Itch Mites

These tiny larval mites live on the ground or in dry logs and are more likely encountered if you are camping. Try to avoid sitting on logs or the ground. The juvenile mites bite, usually in skin folds or areas constricted by clothing such as the waist. The tell-tale sign is a raised red area of skin around the barely visible animal. Intense irritation can follow. Insect repellent should deter them and applied to the attached mites, should kill them. If you get a heavy infestation wash all clothing and bathe to get rid of stray mites.

Ticks

Normally bandicoots and other animals are the hosts for ticks. The most dangerous is the female scrub tick whose toxin can cause paralysis. She is recognisable by being flat with brown legs and long, prominent mouth parts. A headache or nausea may be the sign of a bite. The presence of a tick is mostly recognised by an itchy swelling around the bite area and an application of insecticide or alcohol will cause it to drop off. If pulling the tick off with tweezers, be sure to remove the head which often gets left behind.

Snakes

More likely to be seen trying to get out of your way, snakes are best avoided by looking where you step and where you brush past. Wearing thick socks and long trousers is a precaution. Look out particularly in winter when they are likely to be found lying in open, sunny areas. Not all snakes are venomous but if you are bitten, it will help in your treatment if you can remember what the snake looked like. Apply a tight, broad pressure bandage, keep the affected limb immobile and get the patient to hospital with a minimum of panic.

Estuarine Crocodiles

On the coast, where the rivers run through the rainforest to the sea, is where you are more likely to encounter a crocodile. However, they can be in other low-lying wet places and, indeed, in some out-of-the-way rock pools. If camping in a likely area, pitch your tent away from deep water pools. To bathe or wash-up collect your water from a shallow spot and move away to complete your task. Obviously, swimming in these areas is not recommended.

Freshwater Stonefish

Known as Bullrouts they resemble stones and conceal themselves in weed-beds or among the rocks of coastal streams and rock pools. They have sharp venomous spikes that can pierce soft footwear, so wear hard-soled shoes when walking or swimming in streams. If stung, soaking the foot in hot water relieves the pain, but you should seek medical help if the pain persists.

Slippery Rocks

The major cause of fatalities to rock-hoppers and those who choose the cool mountain streams for a swim are slippery rocks. Take great care, particularly after rain, to avoid a severe knock on the head from a fall or an unexpected dip in a raging torrent.

Cassowaries

If you are lucky enough to encounter a cassowary in places mentioned in this book they will more likely be somewhat accustomed to humans. All the same, never try to feed them and stand near a tree for safety. If they appear to be aggressive, which is possible if they are guarding a nearby nest, then don't run away, rather, stand still or back off slowly to a safe position.

Marine stingers

From October to May the sea is home to deadly marine stingers and box jellyfish which make ocean bathing dangerous. Look for an enclosed stinger net swimming area, a public swimming pool or visit one of the many freshwater swimming spots which are often located near rainforest walking trails.

Lawyer vine

Also known as 'wait-a-while' the tendrils of this plant are sure to find keen walkers at some time or other. To detach yourself, simply pull the barbs back in the reverse order to which they attached themselves. Be careful, particularly, to avoid damage to your eyes. Spines that break off in the skin should be removed with tweezers.

Stinging tree

Known as the gympie gympie, the name is applied to a number of closely related trees of the genus *Dendrocnide*. They are the most likely danger encountered along the rainforest tracks and alongside roads where they grow in response to the extra light. You should always be able to identify this plant. Its heart-shaped leaves and its branches have fine, poisonous hairs that can penetrate skin if you brush past a plant. The sting, which begins as a slight itch and develops into severe pain, may persist for several days and recur for up to two months. If you get a sting, first, don't scratch the spot. If you can, apply and remove sticking plaster or shave the affected area. Also, try flooding the sting with dilute acid, then washing with water to remove the fine hairs.

Rainforest fruits

Many of these make delicious eating and many are poisonous, even fatal. Make sure you identify which is which with a good guide book before attempting to eat or taste any. If you are in doubt it would be best to leave them well alone.

VISITOR CODE

Remember, we are visitors to the forests and the less we disturb the plant and animal life the more chance it will be around in years to come. Basically, the rule is leave the forests as you found them. These fragile and diverse ecosystems need all the help they can get so that visitors do not become part of the problem.

Most importantly, stay on the walking tracks since small plants are easily disturbed and please don't take 'short cuts' through the forest because they can lead to erosion. Please don't pick flowers or other plant material and leave seeds where they lie since they are both the seeds of the future forest and food for animals. If you like the plants why not try growing some of them at home. A number of nurseries specialise in rainforest plants and many tropical species can be grown south of the Wet Tropics.

Just briefly: leave your pets at home; take any rubbish out with you; don't feed the wildlife; and don't pollute the water. As they say, enjoy yourself and: 'leave nothing but footsteps and take nothing but photographs'!

INTRODUCTION

THE WET TROPICS WORLD HERITAGE AREA CONTAINS MUCH OF the tropical rainforest in Australia. Some of these forests contain elements which have persisted from times when this now island continent formed a part of the ancient super-continent Gondwana. Other vegetation resembles closely the forests which existed on the earth up to 100 million years ago. This bioregion of unique flora and fauna easily met the strict criteria for World Heritage listing in 1988.

The magnificent scenery includes mountain ranges, fast flowing streams and waterfalls, deep gorges and dense forests. And, ever present, the rainforest-clad ranges, more often than not the peaks shrouded in cloud, form the backdrop to a spectacular landscape. The Wet Tropics also is the most diverse habitat for flora and fauna in Australia. Many of the plants and animals are unique to the area and some are rare or threatened.

For many people a walk in a shadowy, moist rainforest, with its luxuriant growth, is an overwhelming experience. As the antithesis of the drier open eucalypt forests which have come to be regarded as typically Australian, they often appear strange and foreboding. In fact, it was only at the end of the last century that sclerophyll vegetation became aesthetically acceptable; before that the rainforests were the popular places to visit, especially for jaded urban dwellers escaping the heat and dust of the cities. At the end of this century the old appreciations are returning.

The diversity of plant life is astonishing. Small plants appear to be striving upwards towards the light, while the giant, often buttressed, trees have their head foliage way out of sight, with only fallen leaves or fruit or a knowledge of bark types giving a clue to their identity. From up above, the searching roots of seedling strangler figs drop down, seeking nourishment from the moist soil, to lay a claim on its host tree. The 'gothic' feel of the forest is reinforced when you come across a large fig, with its matted tangle of trunk, standing cathedral-like and dominating its surroundings. All around a multitude of lianes, the ubiquitous wait-a-while, clinging epiphytes and countless varieties of plants compete for attention. On the ground, a variety of mosses, lichens and fungi attack and live on a mass of rotting debris which is being rapidly absorbed back into its surroundings. The myriad of small ferns and, at different times of the year, the variety of flowering plants add to the botanical profusion.

There are many different types of rainforest in the Wet Tropics. And although nearly a third of the Wet Tropics is comprised of vegetation other than rainforest, the bias of this book is towards describing the areas of rainforest.

Variations in rainfall, soil type and drainage, altitude and location lead to forests which you will soon be able to distinguish by recognising the differing plant life. As well, the diversity of flora is incredible with more than 1200 species of rainforest trees alone. Usually, no particular species dominates, while occasionally some are so rare as to be only represented by several examples. Thorough botanical studies are only beginning in many areas and scientists are just starting to document the potential value of pharmaceuticals derived from many plants.

While you walk the forest pathways it is worth being aware that, for thousands of years, several distinct clans of people actually lived within the rainforests, with a culture that was unique in Australia. Very often the sites of Aboriginal significance are remembered to this day and the rich tapestry of mythology which infuses the Wet Tropics adds a special dimension to the region. In many instances, a cultural revival is allowing many of the practical and spiritual aspects to be presented to visitors today.

The Wet Tropics also has a recent past which is equally fascinating and the present-day mosaic of land use is a testament to generations of people from a diverse range of ethnic backgrounds who have toiled against the elements to bring the land into production.

Finally, while visiting the forests is a more benign activity than harvesting them for timber, or indeed clearing them for marginal agricultural pursuits, it is incumbent on us all to ensure that places do not become 'loved to death' in our efforts to enjoy them as sites of recreation. For this reason, nearly all the walks in this book are to places which have adequate facilities for visitors and which have been endorsed by the Wet Tropics Management Authority for people to visit. Enjoy them and 'tread lightly' in the forests.

WHY A WORD HERITAGE AREA

FOUR CRITERIA ARE USED TO ASSESS WHETHER A PARTICULAR area containing natural heritage should be included on the list of World Heritage Areas. The site must: be an outstanding example representing the major stages of the earth's **evolutionary history**; be an outstanding example representing ongoing **ecological processes and biological evolution**; contain **superlative natural phenomena**, formations or features; and contain important and significant natural **habitats for plant and animal threatened species**. The Wet Tropics is exceptional in that it is one of a handful of natural World Heritage sites worldwide that meets all four criteria.

Evolutionary History

Eight major stages in the earth's evolutionary history are represented:
• The Age of Ferns (Pteridophytes);
• The Age of Conifers and Cycads;
• The Age of Flowering Plants (Angiosperms);
• The final break-up of the ancient super-continent of Gondwana;
• Biological evolution and radiation during 35 mill. years of isolation;
• The origin and radiation of the songbirds;
• The mixing of the continental biota of the Australian and Asian
    continental plates; and
• The effects of the Pleistocene glacial periods on tropical rainforest
    vegetation.

These forests are living museums. They contain one of the most complete and diverse living records of the major stages in the evolution of the land plants, from the very first plants on land to the higher plants (gymnosperms and angiosperms). The rainforests are major surviving remnants of the Gondwanan forests of more than 60 million years ago. As the continent became drier, plant genera such as Eucalyptus, Leptospermum and Callistemon evolved from rainforest ancestors, whose oldest relatives are found today in the rainforests of this region.

The closest relatives of the ancient Australian birdlife, which are considered to be the ancestors of many of the world's songbirds, are distributed throughout the Wet Tropics region. The rainforests also contain unique marsupials which are relics of animal life that inhabited the once much more extensive rainforests of the Australian continent. Many other species originated when Australia was part of

Gondwana, including some species of frogs, geckos and insects. Their presence shows that the rainforest habitat has probably existed continuously since ancient times.

Geological Processes and Biological Evolution

The Wet Tropics, which represents 0.1 per cent of Australia's land area, is home to 50 per cent of the bird species, 30 per cent of the marsupial species, 27 per cent of its frog species, 23 per cent of its reptile species and 60 per cent of its butterfly species.

Many of the species live only in small distinct places within the area, they are endemic and found nowhere else in the world. Several exist only as isolated populations but in areas with the same altitude and climate, which means that at times of long-term and global climate change they can relocate and survive if conditions are favourable.

The Wet Tropics also contain the most diverse assemblage of primitive angiosperm families in the world. Of the 19 known families of primitive angiosperms, 13 occur within this area. These living fossils provide unique insights into the early evolution and diversification of the flowering plants. As well, the area contains forest communities considered to have separated from rainforests early in the evolutionary process. Eucalypts that now dominate the Australian landscape are considered to have evolved from rainforest ancestors and spread out into drier environments from the edges of their parent forests.

The Wet Tropics covers a range of altitudes, topography, rainfall and soil types which is generally reflected in the diversity and complexity of the rainforest and associated communities in the region. It is distinguished by dramatic transitions from one vegetation type to another.

Superlative Natural Phenomena

The diversity of landscapes includes not only the various types of rainforests but also other forest vistas which include the surrounding drier eucalypt forests. The boundaries are sometimes distinct and in other places gradual. In some places the rainforest meets the sea with outstanding coastal scenery that combines rainforests, beaches and fringing reefs offshore. The side-by-side relationships of the two World Heritage Areas, the Wet Tropics and the Great Barrier Reef, is unique.

Noah Creek is one of the most significant of all lowland plant refugia. Here there is a great concentration of primitive flowering plants and representatives of some of the most ancient of contemporary plant lineages. Further along the creek from where this photograph was taken is one of the three populations of *Gymnostoma australianum*. This is the most primitive member of the she-oak group or Casuarinaceae which has evolved from rainforest to occupy drier habitats. P. LIK

Habitat for Threatened Species

The Wet Tropics is the principal or only habitat for numerous species of threatened plants and animals that are regarded as rare, vulnerable or endangered. Many species have small, fragmented distributions. Among higher plants only a small percentage of the approximately 3000 species can be regarded as common in the region. Many primitive angiosperm families, for example, are confined to small, wet upland or lowland areas.

There are at least 54 species of vertebrate animals that are regarded as very rare, found only in small areas or in danger of extinction. Endangered or threatened species include the Brush-tailed Bettong, the Spotted-tailed Quoll, the Mahogany Glider, the northern race of the Yellow-bellied Glider (the Fluffy Glider) and the Southern Cassowary. Several other species of animals have very restricted distribution, including: the Atherton Antechinus and Thornton Peak Melomys and various frogs and reptiles. The Golden-tipped Bat is also rare and was thought to be extinct until it was rediscovered in the Cairns region in 1981. There are seven species of frog, all of which are confined to the region, which have suffered recent declines and some may now well be extinct.

ABORIGINAL LIFE IN THE RAINFOREST

AT THE TIME OF FIRST CONTACT IN THE NINETEENTH-CENTURY the area now called the Wet Tropics was the home of 16 different tribal groups of Aboriginal people. They lived as clans of 20–25 individuals and a number of clans would make up a tribe of about 250 people. Thatched huts were constructed for homes in the Wet Season, either in clearings or on the edges of forests. In winter the people made use of blankets formed from the bark of fig trees.

The forests were rich enough in plant and animal resources to be able to provide food for a relatively high population density. These people had a primarily vegetarian diet, derived almost entirely from the rainforests, which included hundreds of different plants varied occasionally by the flesh of animals such as wallabies, tree-kangaroos, fish, birds, and possums. Some of the nuts and roots they eat were toxic in their raw state, and these were pounded up and placed in dilly-bags in running water for several days to leach the toxins out. It was this ability to process some of their potential foods which enabled people to survive times of food shortages. Pathways through the forest were the routes of travel and trade that formed the basis of the social system.

It is easy to assume that the people led an idyllic existence. Late last century W.H. Miskin noted of the people of the South Johnstone River district:

> The quantity and variety of fruits, nuts and roots in this vast garden of nature, and the numerous streams teeming with fish with which this country is so lavishly endowed, and shell-fish on the coast, provides them with an easily acquired and abundant living.

But this glowing assessment of the abundance of food needs to be tempered by the realisation that times of food shortages would have been common after cyclonic weather and in seasonal dry times. During extreme wet seasons, when there was a lack of food in the forests, the people often moved to more open country. Mostly, however, they had main camps, with a supply of stored food, to live in during this time. In the cool dry winters the people were more mobile, particularly towards the start of the Wet Season when food was plentiful and when social interaction was at a peak. It was at this time that the dramatic dancing and fighting corroborees took place.

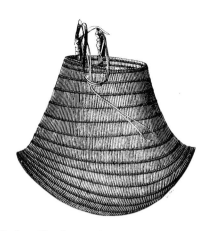

Baskets like this one from the Herbert River district have been used to carry possessions and to leach the toxins from pounded seeds.

The material culture of the people was unique with women making elaborate string bags and men weaving distinctive baskets braided from lawyer cane. Shields were manufactured from the buttresses of trees and decorated in bold geometric designs which distinguished different groups. As well, large wooden swords, requiring two hands to wield, were used in warfare and ceremony. For many of the tribes these were the only weapons they used as the dense rainforest vegetation often precluded the successful use of spears and, more particularly, boomerangs.

Like people from other parts of the continent they practiced a degree of cannibalism. But, on the evidence presented by most white observers, it appears to have been infrequent and primarily non-ritualistic. As well, bodies were often mummified before cremation and fighting corroborees were often held to settle disputes between tribes. It was here that the distinctive weapons came into use although fighting was more often ritualistic than fully intensive. 'Mortal wounds are extremely rare' noted the naturalist Carl Lumholtz, and if someone was in danger it was often the women who would interfere to prevent someone from getting wounded.

In the Herbert River district a system of net hunting was also observed by Lumholtz. As well, he noted the method of burning adjacent grasslands to flush out the game that would then be speared or clubbed. In all areas different species of possum were important foods as were flying fox and many birds such as the Brush-turkey *(Alectura lathami)* and various waterfowl. A method of fishing was to place bark from the Foambark *(Jagera pseudorhus)* in a waterhole and wait for the chemical reaction to cause the stunned fish to float to the surface.

Fire was a powerful tool used to not only force wildlife into the open, but also to later attract it when the fresh shoots sprang up. This activity, combined with changing climatic conditions, restricted rainforests to favourable sites and encouraged the expansion of the more fire resistant eucalypt and acacia vegetation. Ironically, it was the complex land management practices of the Aborigines which produced the 'wilderness' that early European explorers and settlers were so intent on 'discovering' and categorising.

The coming of Europeans

When Phillip King anchored at Rockingham Bay in June 1819 on his coastal expedition, he was met by men in small bark canoes. These people were welcomed on deck where there was an exchange of artifacts. Later, a party from the ship visited the huts of the local tribe where they observed their material culture, including stone 'ovens' used for cooking. Farther north at the inlet to the Bloomfield River

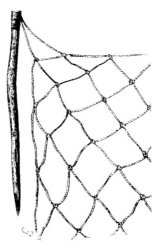

Fishing nets were woven from forest fibres.

one of the crew went ashore and found a canoe, seven metres long, carved out of a tree trunk and fitted with an outrigger.

In many cases it was Aboriginal guides who led expeditions into and through rainforested regions for both exploration and settlement. The most celebrated were Edmund Kennedy's assistant Galmarra, and Christie Palmerston's guide Pompo, but others helped to open up large areas that eventually became cleared for settlement. More often it was Aborigines who knew the best places to spot the unique foliage of the red cedars which were prized by the timber-getters. Palmerston used men from the local tribes as porters to carry his supplies on gold finding expeditions. Often it was the Aboriginal pathways through the rainforest that facilitated the exploration of areas.

Carl Lumholtz would not have found one of the regions' two species of rare tree-kangaroos without the benefit of local knowledge. And early settlers acknowledged that hundreds of lives were saved by Aboriginal trackers who directed searches in the often impenetrable rainforest vegetation.

At first the people were able to accommodate the new arrivals to some extent by moving into uncleared forest. As Lumholtz observed:

> In these picturesque but very inaccessible scrubs the natives live in large numbers undisturbed by the white man, for there is no gold or other treasure to tempt him to subject himself to all the inconveniences connected with the effort to penetrate into these regions.

The more remote rainforests were both a home and a refuge in regions

Fashioned from the buttress roots of various rainforest trees, these shields, with distinctive geometrical patterns, were used in ritual warfare.

that were the last to experience the effects of white settlement. But as the people were forced to retreat to the inaccessible areas they lost the use of their full range of habitats. The lowland forests, which were the first to be taken, contained plants and game that were essential in their seasonal patterns of food gathering. A local police commissioner was to report in 1878 that 'the natives were literally starving'. This deprivation no doubt precipitated the desperate actions that by all accounts led to a situation of frontier warfare in many districts. Aboriginal resistance and, increasingly, raids on the white settlers were mostly carried out from the concealment of the rainforests. Christie Palmerston boasted of his many skirmishes; 'Thin shields may answer very well for the purpose of their wars, but my rifle drilled them as if they were sheets of paper'.

While observers like Lumholtz and others provided valuable insights into the more obvious aspects of Aboriginal life in the rainforests, the perspective is often clouded by prejudice and ethnocentricity. Lumholtz could not accept that Aborigines had unique ways of seeing their physical surroundings. He reflected: 'the scenery is simply overwhelming in its splendour, and yet there is no one to admire all this beauty save the blacks, who do not comprehend it!'. The original inhabitants were rarely perceived as being able to appreciate their environment.

One of the most perceptive observers of the people in the rainforests was the Swedish naturalist and anthropologist Eric Mjöberg, who spent a year in the Atherton district in 1912-1913. Although the railway had arrived at the Tableland and clearing was well advanced, he found several groups of people still living traditional lifestyles in the Tully River and Cedar Creek areas. Relying on, and adding to, the ethnographical research begun 10 years earlier by Walter Roth, Mjöberg regarded the people he came in contact with as the most skillful hunters and fishers in the world. He also observed the buttress roots of trees being used like drums for communication and that they cut shields from them.

He was also particularly impressed with the way older people in the groups he visited were 'cherished and looked after', being appreciated especially for their wisdom and experience. Mjöberg felt very strongly that the mission system was failing to improve the life of remnant tribes of the rainforest. Their religion, he realised, was so different to that of the Europeans that it was impossible to judge one better than the other. Due to the reluctance of his informants he was not able to find out much about their spiritual world. With an insight rare among his contemporaries, Mjöberg thought the missionaries, who were more concerned with religion than the practicable, had only changed the people on the surface. 'At the bottom of their soul there is still superstition and spirituality', he noted, adding 'This is what makes them special'.

Revival

Archaeologists are really only beginning to research rainforest prehistory. One of the major sites under investigation is Jiyer Cave a rockshelter in the Russell River valley. Preliminary results suggest occupations dating back several thousand years but exact dates for rainforest occupation are difficult to ascertain because the region's high temperatures, humidity and rainfall mean that remains of material cultures do not survive for long. And finding sites in the rugged terrain of the remaining natural areas is no mean task. Much research could be carried out by asking the Aboriginal people themselves. In the Atherton Tableland their legends appear to correlate to the scientific view of the

---

With bodies painted and weaponry ready, the men and boys in this photograph have prepared themselves for a ceremonial dance. A large rainforest sword can be seen on the left, while a variety of shields are evident. This image is from *Among the Stoneage People in Queensland's Wilderness* by Swedish anthropologist Eric Mjöberg.

previous open vegetation on the Tableland, before volcanic activity changed the vegetation to rainforest.

Today, while most people do not live within the rainforests, there are many communities which still regard these places highly for their spiritual values and who still have their culture and language intact. They have not forgotten the important sites which they continue to visit. For many, ties with the past have been combined with contemporary life to make the best of 'two worlds'.

There has also been a recent revival in aspects of rainforest culture which includes the making of artefacts and reviving the knowledge of plant usage. This is being passed on to interested visitors, often through indigenous tour ventures. An insight into Aboriginal perspectives of the rainforests gives the visitor increased powers of observation and a new way of seeing these unique ecosystems.

THE NEW SETTLERS

DESPITE PRODUCING DETAILED MAPS OF THE NORTH QUEENSLAND coastline, early explorers such as James Cook (1770), Matthew Flinders (1802) and Phillip King (1819) all failed to note the extent of the rainforests that clothed the mountain sides and plains, often right down to the sea-shore. Land exploration in the region began with Ludwig Leichhardt's epic journey from Moreton Bay to Port Essington in 1844–45. Travelling west of the Great Dividing Range, his journal was able to offer little assistance to Edmund Kennedy when he was planning his ill-fated journey which started a few years later.

It was not until the early 1870s, when George Dalrymple was commissioned to explore the coast between Cardwell and the Endeavour River, that settlement followed. In 1864 he had sailed for Rockingham Bay to survey a route south-west across the heavily rainforested Cardwell and Seaview ranges to the Upper Burdekin. His party had good relations with the Aborigines who, 15 years earlier, had skirmished with Kennedy's expedition and he succeeded in establishing a rough track inland. The pastoral boom had slackened by the end of the decade, but the potential for tropical agriculture on the coast and adjacent tableland north of Cardwell was soon to be realised. His subsequent report, exclaiming the potential of the Johnstone River region, was formed by his experience in tropical agriculture and was influential in attracting new settlers. For Dalrymple, the region was a 'Northern Eldorado' with the luxuriant vegetation implying good soil fertility, and that only clearing of the 'dark dank jungles' and the dispersal of their 'wild inhabitants' were necessary before prosperity was brought to the region.

It was the coastal rainforests that were to prove most daunting to William Hann's 1872 expedition which ventured further north into Cape York and which returned south along the east coast from successfully traversing, mapping and describing a wide area at the base of the Peninsula. However, he found the steep and rugged slopes of the Cape Tribulation area almost impossible to traverse: 'the eye rested on hills and scrub everywhere, there was not the ghost of a chance of finding a track to tread these mazes, and to endeavour to penetrate them would have been madness'. Deciding to turn back and head inland, he wrote frustratingly of the 'completely impassible nature of the country for white men with horses'.

Timber getting

From the beginning of white settlement the land was expected to be adaptable for most types of primary production, regardless of the methods adopted. There was also considered to be enough resources in the forests to supply all timber needs. Just how and why this apparent abundance was squandered is partly explained by examining the record of rainforest deforestation.

Unencumbered land which could support primary production was a necessary prerequisite for attracting migrants and investment capital. The rainforests were not initially selected because the earliest settlers preferred land which was relatively open and free from dense vegetation. They were primarily interested in its grazing potential. Other agricultural pursuits on a large scale were not considered at this time as there were no markets for the produce, at least within the colony. As the population increased the last great frontier for small settlers was the rainforests.

Economic exploitation of the rainforests began with the timber-cutters who searched the forests of the mountain ranges and coastal river systems for Red Cedar *(Toona ciliata)*. The timber from this tree was highly prized for furniture and joinery. A reasonably abundant tree, it was sought from southern New South Wales to Cooktown after land exploration expeditions progressively reported new areas of rainforest. The cedar forests were being cut on the Johnstone and Daintree Rivers in the 1870s and the following decade on the Atherton Tableland. By the 1890s the cedar was largely cut out, although it was still being logged in smaller quantities well into the twentieth-century.

As land was thrown open for settlement the pace of timber harvesting was stepped up. The resulting glut of logs meant that

This engraving of Edmund Kennedy and an assistant at the start of his expedition catches the optimism that was present after the original landing.
After a sketch by T.H. Huxley.

valuable species were often used for the most utilitarian of purposes or that logs were often left to rot on the ground for lack of markets. The difficulty in transporting the resource to market, combined with the disorderly timber marketing system and rampant land speculation, brought enormous pressures on the forests. Nevertheless, the timber trade was the most important economy of many newly opened lands, particularly on the Atherton Tableland in the early part of this century. As dealers and speculators vied for the land they often took advantage of selectors who had little idea of the timber value of the rainforest on their land. The newly-formed forestry service could do little to halt the devastation.

These timber fellers are posing for the photographer before completing the herculean task of felling this large fig tree.

Within the government there was conflict between the emerging forestry profession, which was becoming alarmed at the situation, and the Lands Department which was busy opening land to settlement with little regard for conservation principles, land economics or appropriate land utilisation. The system of trial and error for potential land use by settlers with no farming experience led to a chaotic situation which came to head in 1931 with the appointment of a Royal Commission to attempt to resolve the conflict between land settlement and forestry. The subsequent report was biased in favour of land settlement and the unsatisfactory situation more or less continued. Foresters found themselves with a diminishing resource, with which they had to manage the increasing demands for a supply of timber with the necessity to keep the forests intact for new cutting cycles.

From the 1930s through to after World War II new technology allowed for an expansion of veneer and plywood manufacture. With the cutting out of prime cabinetwoods the value of many of the previously unused species was also recognised and a sawlog industry developed on this trade. In 1948 quotas were introduced to help regulate the industry, but since they were based on the high volumes of the post-war years, they were too high to ensure long-term timber harvesting at these rates. When it was obvious that the resource would soon be exhausted, the call for sustained yield timber cutting was met with significantly reduced quotas in 1978. Despite this, harvesting was allowed to continue at an unsustainable rate and trees that were hundreds of years old were felled with little regard for the ecological consequences.

Mining

In the early 1870s the Palmer River goldfields attracted the attention of thousands of would-be miners who sluiced the rivers and streams for the precious metal. As the last great popular gold rush in Australia, the Palmer fields were mined under chaotic conditions in the northern extremes of climate. Later it was tin that brought the prospectors.

Conditions on the fields were rough and ready with the law of the frontier often applying to disputes between the diggers. There were also skirmishes with local Aborigines who resented the massive intrusion that went with the new finds. As well, a large contingent of Chinese miners worked the Palmer and other goldfields. Often precluded from new fields their successes were often the result of patiently working over abandoned claims for payable gold. They were, however, subject to much discrimination and were eventually chased off many fields. Harsh legislation, which restricted their activities, forced many people back to their homeland.

Most of the gold and tin mining occurred in the area north of the Bloomfield River; near China Camp and Gold Hill on the McDowall Range; at Tinaroo Creek on the Atherton; at the Mulgrave, Russell, Johnstone and Tully River headwaters; at the Cardwell Range, Mt Fox, Kangaroo Hill and at Mt Spec.

By the end of the nineteenth-century most of the easily accessible minerals were claimed and heavy-duty machinery was brought in to crush the ore from which more gold and tin was extracted. Today it is possible to literally stumble on holes in the ground in some parts of the Wet Tropics that prospectors have long abandoned and which have been reclaimed by regrowth forest.

Agriculture

When the rushes were over many diggers turned to agricultural pursuits for a means of living. Extra pressures were now put on the rainforests, not so much by an increased demand for timber, but as potential land for small holdings. Early selective logging was never as comparably damaging as the later wholesale clearing. The demands on the previously uncleared mountain forest were exacerbated by new laws designed to encourage settlement. Rainforests fell to the axe and fire-stick as closer settlement acts favoured small-scale farming. One early writer explained how the forest was cleared:

> First the smaller shrubbery and creepers are prostrated with the axe and bill hooks, [at] a time of the year when a few months of dry weather may be expected... When the stuff thus levelled is pretty thoroughly sun-dried, the trees of magnitude are now attacked with axe, and for the bulkiest, cross-cut saw... When in their turn the large trees are ascertained to be well dried, a windy day is chosen and fire applied. If the season has been favourable for drying, the result is splendid.

Often those that lacked the capital or desire to cultivate their land would find a tenant prepared to take up a 'clearing lease', whereby, for a modest rent, the lessee would clear and farm the land for a specified time, usually five years. After then the forest vegetation and the stumps had rotted and the land was fit for ploughing. Many of these leases were taken by Chinese farmers who were not allowed to own freehold land. For the landowner, who would often have a job elsewhere, it was an effortless way of clearing their properties.

Pastoral expansion followed Leichhardt's inland route and through the 1860s settlers took up land between Bowen on the coast and the Gulf of Carpentaria. The majority of settlement on the coast, however, dates from the 1880s and later. The first commercial crop was sugar which led to the alienation and clearing of much of the lowland rain-

---

Clearing the vast tropical lowland rainforests was well underway by the 1880s. The flat arable land was recognised as suitable for sugar cane growing and with the advent of a regular shipping service markets were developed in the south.

forest. The Atherton Tableland was slower to develop because of doubts over suitable crops and the poor transport situation. The most valuable asset of the land was more often the prime cabinet timber trees which were much sought after since their depletion in other areas. However, often valuable forests were just felled and burnt as land clearing became more intense around the turn of the century.

It was always assumed that the profuse vegetation of the rainforests was supported by soils of great fertility. The incentive to clear them was no doubt based on this apparent fact. As it turned out, apart from the natural fertility of the basalt derived soils, the rainforest was more often than not sustained by its own closed cycle of fertility which resulted from rotting vegetation and humus that was constantly being provided by the mass of vegetation. When this cycle was broken by removing the vegetation the soils soon lost their inherent fertility and cleared land was often abandoned to a regrowth of weeds and saplings. When Ellis Rowan visited Cairns late last century she thought it a 'sacrilege to cut down the beautiful timber' and observing the paddocks of sugar cane she lamented the 'gaunt skeletons of ringed trees' standing out against the sky like 'grim sentinels at their post'.

The arguments concerning the suitability of European labour in tropical regions was a constant topic for discussion when white settlement was underway in north Queensland. In 1885, the naturalist W.H. Miskin enthused about the 'interminable' expanse of the region's rainforest which he thought covered 'probably the richest and most fertile soil in the world'. He suggested that it was:

> awaiting only a more enlightened public policy towards the tropical agricultural industry to realise wealth to the enterprising capitalist, and profitable employment to thousands of human beings; but now lying, and apparently for some time likely to do so, absolutely worthless − a wilderness of waste.

Miskin considered it impracticable for white people to be employed in the clearing of rainforests as there was 'no single instance' in the world where there was successful white settlement in tropical zones. He envisioned the large-scale importation of 'a suitable class of agricultural labour' because 'the white race…unless constantly replenished by an ever-continuous influx of immigration from temperate climes, gradually degenerate from the parent stock, both in physique and civilisation'. This argument was used by owners of large sugar plantations to initiate a trade in indentured labour from the Pacific Islands as a workforce for the sugar cane fields. The introduction of Kanakas, as they were called, was resented by white workers who saw their livelihood threatened. Other people were concerned at the development of what was virtually a slave trade. Before the scheme was abandoned at the turn of the century, thousands of Melanesian and Polynesian workers provided a cheap means of consolidating a profitable sugar industry.

Sugar was the boom crop of the early 1880s and the major crop planted in place of the lowland rainforests was sugar cane. Encouraged by liberal land selection laws from the early 1870s, prospective emigrants were being induced to select rainforested land because 'the soil which has been able to foster the growth of a thick scrub... is more likely to be able to grow sugar cane'. Because sugar cane grew for 18 months before harvest, tobacco or potatoes would often be

Carl Lumholtz, the Norwegian zoologist, searched the Herbert River Valley late last century for the 'Boongerry'. Eventually found by his Aboriginal companions, the tree-kangaroo was to be named after him.

planted to give an early return. One observer noted with regret that each year the intervening 'dark patches of primeval scrub...grow less, and more and more of the soil is put under sugar'. Bananas were another successful crop and these and exotic fruit trees were cultivated by waves of new settlers. The Chinese often settled to work the land while, later on, it was Italian farmers, beginning as cane cutters, who eventually took up their own farms.

The pace of settlement was hampered by Aboriginal resistance on the frontier. From the settlers' point of view the threat of attacks from the surrounding forests was real. In 1880 a selector wrote to the Herberton Advertiser describing his fear: 'When we go to work, [we] have to go armed carrying our lives in our hands; and when engaged in falling scrub, or doing any other work are liable to be speared or tomahawked any moment'.

Later on dairying was to become another important industry, particularly on the Tableland which was opened for wider settlement from

1903 when the railway line was completed. It was this industry which ensured the closer settlement ideal of the time could become a reality. Eventually, many of the cleared areas reverted to marginal grazing land where beef cattle were fattened on improved pastures. Often farmers employed primitive firestick methods which ensured open paddocks, but which pushed the rainforest boundaries back a small way each year. Meanwhile, the hillsides were infested with weeds and regrowth rainforest or else tended to slip away after torrential rainfall.

Today, wiser land uses are prevailing with a surprising variety of crops being grown and marginal land is often reforested by local tree-planting groups or by the Wet Tropics Management Authority.

Tourism and conservation

Rainforests were always valued as places for city people to visit on day trips, especially those which were close to major towns and cities. The first national parks in Queensland protected areas of rainforest, often around particular scenic features such as waterfalls, grand vistas, 'ferny dells' or cool mountain forests. Many of these areas became the Australian equivalent of the Indian 'hill stations' where usually well-off people would spend the hot months relaxing or tending gardens that they would reclaim from the 'wilderness'. Eventually, the increasing middle classes were quick to follow with their day trips made possible by the expansion of the rail system to favoured places.

Recreation and aesthetics, rather than conservation, were originally the main reasons for preserving the rainforests. However, scientific expeditions had been mounted which collected plant and animal specimens from the rainforests and although their potential resource

The forest clearing that was associated with the Cape Tribulation–Bloomfield road was extremely damaging to the coastal ecosystem.

Proposals to turn the road into a walking track with a boat service linking the two communities of Cape Tribulation and Bloomfield would help create a world-class attraction.   M. GRAHAM

values were always scrutinised, there was great interest when new species were discovered.

The rise of ecology as a discipline in the last 30 years has focussed attention on various types of vegetation and especially rainforest. Scientists began to see the forests not only as a treasure-trove of flora and fauna but also as the clue to the evolution of species.

Conservation groups began to press their claims for forest protection as an awareness that the unsustainable rate of logging was threatening to degrade the areas that had escaped the settlers' clearing. When the local council began to reopen an old road and extend it through to the Bloomfield River in late 1983, the action provoked a

A postcard from the turn of the last century which shows the Barron Falls at flood-time before the Hydro Station.

blockade by protesters. Despite drawing nationwide attention to the issue, the blockaders were removed by police and the road completed a year later. Further pressures from loggers to access some of the remaining forests in the area led to a campaign to stop logging. Despite world-wide concern and imminent World Heritage listing, the government of the day decided to step-up logging in some areas while negotiations continued. Eventually, all rainforest logging was stopped and displaced workers were offered alternative work and re-training, while timber mills were compensated for the loss of resource.

World Heritage listing over the massive 8900 km^2 forest domain was gained in 1988. The task of managing the mosaic of land uses, while implementing the listing's obligations of protection, conservation and presentation, was entrusted to the Wet Tropics Management Authority formed in 1990. In recent years tourism is providing more economic benefits to local communities than timber harvesting could in its dying days. Only time, and good planning, will tell if this industry is compatible with the long-term survival of Australia's tropical rainforests.

PHOTOGRAPHY IN THE RAINFOREST

People who appreciate the rainforest scenes reproduced in publications often wonder about the photographic techniques which were used to capture them. It has even been suggested that the images of misty mountain tops, wild gorge scenery and feathery flowing streams running over moss-covered boulders are more attractive than a visitor's actual experiences in the rainforests. However, with some preparation, patience and planning, it is possible to capture both the immenseness of the scenery as well as the minutiae which goes to make up the total experience of the Wet Tropics.

Camera, lenses and accessories

A basic 35 mm camera is fine, preferably one which allows you to override the suggested camera settings as dictated by the lightmeter. You will want to limit your gear somewhat unless you can persuade a friend to carry excess baggage, but some things are essential besides the camera and appropriate film. A tripod is one, because in low light situations where exposures can be as low as one second, it is impossible to hold the camera steady. And a cable shutter release or self-timer will keep the camera rock steady when you trip the shutter.

Wide-angle lenses are of great value in the rainforest where their wide field-of-view helps to place the wall of greenery effectively in a single frame. And in setting an extended depth-of-field, both the near and far objects will be in focus. Zoom lenses up to 300 mm are also useful if you wish to get close to special plants or if you get lucky enough to see a distant animal which would otherwise be lost in the picture.

Realistically, it is best to be in one photographic mode or another. If you are after views have the right lens in place and look out for good shots with the right lighting. Wildlife photography requires a suitable camera set-up with a thorough knowledge of all controls to minimise mucking around when a situation presents itself. It can also involve long waits in a 'hide' for animals to come into view.

Since the environment can be wet and humid it is wise to keep your gear protected and dry. Some modern electronic cameras will have difficulty operating effectively in these conditions. An umbrella can also come in handy. And remember to carry spare batteries and enough of your special film because you are unlikely to obtain these in the small towns on the periphery of the Wet Tropics.

Film

The most satisfying photography is with slides. New technology even allows get them put on a CD for

Stream beds are good subject matter for photography. These places support the growth of some of the more primitive and water-dependent land plants. They are miniature gardens composed of a great variety of mosses and ferns.   R. RITCHIE

viewing through a special player on your video. They are also most readily accepted for publication. Having said this, don't be put off from taking snaps with print film because if you follow some of the tips mentioned here they will still be of a superior quality. And if you don't have a tripod, use 400 ASA film in low-light interior shots of rainforest. Just be aware that your colours will not be as realistic.

Slide users will most probably be drawn into the Fujichrome/ Kodachrome debate. The professional versions of Fujichrome known as Velvia and Provia have a reputation for dazzling and lush greens. However, they are expensive and require practice for best results. Kodachrome is sharp and the results are fairly predictable but they do pale in comparison to a good Velvia scene when shooting within the rainforest. Some consider Kodachrome more 'natural' in its representation of the scene. Certainly this film is more suitable for landscape photography where the colour distortion of Velvia is not as acceptable. Generally, if you are using a tripod anyway, there is no point in using the faster 100 ASA+ films, so go for sharpness and quality as provided by such films as Kodachrome 25 or Velvia 50 and form your own opinions.

Techniques

What your eye sees is not always what your camera will record. Rainforests can be difficult to photograph because it is impossible to 'get back far enough' and because of tricky or non-existent natural lighting. Patches of strong sunlight need to be avoided since the contrast between areas in full sun and shade are too great for most film to record an even exposure. If your main subject falls in a patch of light, the surrounding shaded area will be too dark (over exposed) in the final image. If you choose to override your light-meter then you get a washed out (over exposed) bright patch. It is best to photograph rainforest interiors in periods of light cloud when there is a strong but muted light source.

As well, early morning or late afternoon will provide an occasion when the scene is highlighted from a low light source which does not cast as many shadows. And closing one eye is a simple technique to use to see if the scene is going to 'work' in two dimensions.

In the open, at lookouts and for panoramas, you can have the opposite problem of too much light, particularly if you have a lot of sky in the shot. Here you should underexpose slightly to compensate. Again, early or late in the day will give you best lighting conditions.

To catch those feathery water effects, place the camera on the tripod low near a creek or cascade so that the movement of the water traverses the scene in the viewfinder from one side to the other, or top to bottom. Make sure the camera is level relative to

Photographers with an eye for detail will also find subject matter by simply being observant. Here the forest floor provides inspiration.　　　　　　P. LIK

the scene and avoid patches of bright sky. Ideally there should be no breeze to disturb leaves and branches. Select an exposure that prioritises a small aperture (ie f8, f11 or smaller) which will then dictate a slow shutter speed of perhaps 1/4 or 1/2 of a second. Depress the shutter ensuring the camera is not jarred and a first rate picture should be yours.

Close-ups make for excellent shots and they are often the easiest to take. Look out for unusual plants, flowers, fungi or obliging insects. Fallen fruits and leaves also make good subjects. Most lenses have a macro facility or it is possible to get simple screw-on lenses which will magnify the scene.

A flash is handy to have in conjunction with a macro/close-up facility. Get to know your flash/lens combination through experimentation. Diffused flashlight can also improve colour, detail and depth-of-field by allowing smaller aperture openings. Often good sunlight can substitute for a flash, it will just depend on the situation. The closer you get the shallower the depth-of-field so try to get the subject's features in focus in a parallel plane to that of the film plane. However, don't worry if the background is out of focus. Remember also that even a slight wind will affect the sharpness of the final image.

Wildlife photography is one of the most difficult of arts to perfect and the images of the type you see in this book were all taken by people who have been both patient and meticulous in their preparation and have been working on their techniques for years.

Such factors as a knowledge of an animal's behaviour including the times they are active, their feeding, breeding and nesting habits and their range are all part of the equation. As a general rule, animals will be found feeding in the early morning or late evening but you need to overcome their shyness and their natural instincts of awareness to strangers to get a good shot. Their acute senses of sight, sound and smell all combine to detect your presence. A good telephoto lens is essential and a tripod will be required.

If you really wish to get serious about your photography keep a written record of the various settings of your camera for each individual photograph. When you get them back from processing write the details on each slide or print and you will soon learn the best settings.

Finally, remember the professionals' secret. Take one or two shots under and over the recommended exposure settings and you will be surprised how often it is one of these images which turns out to be perfect.

WET TROPICS PLANT BIODIVERSITY

AILA KETO & KEITH SCOTT

The evolution of flowering plants

The emergence of the flowering plants (angiosperms) some 200 million years after the first appearance of the conifers and cycads (gymnosperms) marked the beginning of one of the most fundamental changes in biological diversity on the planet. By about 70 million years ago, gymnosperms had largely been replaced by angiosperms, although the beginnings of the modern flora did not emerge until the Tertiary (65–1.65 million years ago). The current estimates of 235,000 species of flowering plants represents nearly 90 per cent of all plant species on Earth. The Wet Tropics has outstanding significance in relation to the evolution of the flowering plants.

Australia was once part of the southern supercontinent Gondwana. Other parts of that landmass were made up of the continents now known as Africa and South America (West Gondwana) and Antarctica, the subcontinent of India and the island fragments including New Zealand, New Caledonia, New Guinea and Madagascar. Australia, New Zealand and New Guinea were part of East Gondwana.

The origin of the flowering plants is one of the major unsolved questions of botany. East Gondwanan countries are known to contain the greatest concentration of archaic and relict groups relating to the origins of flowering plants. On the other hand, there is a degree of consensus among scientists that the flowering plants first appeared in West Gondwana. The distribution of relict taxa in the individual continents reflects the timing of origin and spread of the different plant groups in relation to the rifting and drifting of continents once part of Gondwana. Evidence suggests that diversification occurred quite rapidly and that a significant number of groups had arisen before the break-up of Gondwana began about 120 million years ago. By this stage, angiosperms had appeared in the northern hemisphere and in

Mesophyll vineforest dominated by the feather palms *Archontophoenix alexandrae* in Cape Tribulation National Park is a relatively rare occurrence since practically all of this forest type has been cleared on the coastal plain. These communities develop best on gritty or gravelly soils with moderate amounts of nutrients and where drainage is poor. P. LIK

South America and Southeast Gondwana (Antarctica and Australasia) and were apparently spreading in two essentially separate, diversifying streams. A significant part of the southern stream became essentially isolated in Australia when, about 50 million years ago, it finally broke away from Antarctica and rafted towards the tropics.

However, distributed throughout the Indo-Pacific regions are numerous fragments, or terranes, derived from the northern margin of the Australian section of Gondwana. These fragments now form parts of South-east Asia, Indonesia and some Pacific islands. It has been suggested that those terranes that rifted during the Cretaceous (131–65 million years ago) when angiosperms first evolved, acted as 'arks', carrying with them an evolving Gondwanan angiosperm flora.

The radiation of floras, as recorded in the fossil record, has occurred in discrete waves. The Australian Wet Tropics region contains outstanding examples representing five major elements in the history of the angiosperms.

The first recognizable angiosperm pollen was *Clavatipollenites hughesii* described from 110-million year-old deposits in southern England. It has also been found in southern Australia from the same time period at Koonwarra in Victoria. It closely resembles the pollen of the living New Caledonian genus *Ascarina* and *Austrobaileya scandens*, a vigorous climbing plant found only in the Wet Tropics.

The most primitive and ancient orders of living flowering plants are the Magnoliales and Laurales. Of the 19 angiosperm families described as the most primitive, 12 occur in the Wet Tropics, giving it the highest concentration of such families on earth. These families are Annonaceae, Austrobaileyaceae, Eupomatiaceae, Himantandraceae, Myristicaceae and Winteraceae in the order Magnoliales and Atherospermataceae, Gyrocarpaceae, Hernandiaceae, Idiospermaceae, Lauraceae and Monimiaceae in the order Laurales.

Of these families, the Austrobaileyaceae, Eupomatiaceae, Idiospermaceae and Himantandraceae are small, relict and virtually extinct and the Wet Tropics is their centre of survival. Austrobaileyaceae and Idiospermaceae, each with just one species in the family (*Austrobaileya scandens* and *Idiospermum australiense*), are found only in the Wet Tropics. Eupomatiaceae and Himantandraceae, with just two species each, extend outside Australia, only to New Guinea and East Malesia (the Moluccas), respectively. They are probably the last few remnants of an ancient assemblage that have survived the attrition of rainforest during dry cycles of the last Ice Ages. *Eupomatia* fossils derive from the Cretaceous and have been discovered in North

America indicating a formerly much larger range.

One of the most sudden and significant transformations of terrestrial plant life occurred about 100 million years ago, leading to a vast and rapid spread of flowering plants throughout the world. Catastrophic events around the Cretaceous–Tertiary boundary (66.5 million years ago) led to major extinctions of flowering plant groups. An estimated 75 per cent of all living species were lost, particularly in the northern hemisphere. However, East Gondwana in the southern hemisphere was relatively unaffected, and consequently the highest concentrations of Cretaceous angiosperm families survived in that region, many of which were still present on the Australian landmass when it finally broke away from Antarctica. Today, the highest concentrations of relict groups from these ancient flowering plant families survive in the Wet Tropics. Cretaceous families include the Cunoniaceae, Proteaceae, Winteraceae, Myrtaceae, Monimiaceae, Rutaceae, Platanaceae, Sapindaceae, Aquifoliaceae, Callitrichaceae, Chloranthaceae, Gunneraceae, Trimeniaceae, Epacridaceae, Olacaceae and Loranthaceae.

East Gondwana (Australia, New Guinea, New Zealand and New Caledonia) was a key area for the early radiations of flowering plants. Significant numbers of groups believed to have originated in East Gondwana still survive in rainforests within these areas, and the Wet Tropics has a special position as the area with the longest continuous history as part of the parent landmass. Forty-three families and 153 genera of flowering plants believed to have originated in East Gondwana are found in the Wet Tropics.

The origins of the modern Australian flora

The final stage in the break-up of Gondwana had a profound effect on global climates and consequently on the evolution of all subsequent life forms. When Australia was still attached to Antarctica, warm equatorial currents reaching polewards ensured a generally more equably wet and warm climate. The detachment and northward drift of the Australian continent allowed the development of circumpolar currents. Temperature gradients between the equator and the poles increased dramatically and the Antarctic ice cap began to form. Forest types once mixed or closely juxtaposed now mostly became geographically separated and extensive regional extinctions of species occurred.

However, the effects of global cooling and accompanying aridity were maximally compensated for in the Wet Tropics region by the northward drift of Australia towards the tropics. As a consequence of this and a wide range of available altitudinal gradients, the Wet Tropics of Queensland is the only large part of the entire Australasian region where rainforests have persisted continuously since Gondwanan times, preserving in the living flora the closest modern-day counterpart of the Gondwanan forests.

Australia was an isolated landmass during several million critical years when today's flora was being shaped. Climate change was a major influencing factor. After separation of the Australian landmass from Antarctica and during its isolated drift towards the equator, there was a general increase in aridity. At this time, major evolutionary radiations took place within the flora, particularly in the plant families Proteaceae, Myrtaceae, Casuarinaceae, Epacridaceae and Rutaceae, and within the marsupials. The Wet Tropics region contains the highest concentration of the surviving remnants of the ancestral stock from which evolved the sclerophyll flora (and marsupial fauna) that now dominate the Australian landscape.

Primitive genera of the Proteaceae, the remnants of ancient Gondwanan origins, are found in the Wet Tropics. In this family that now comprises a very important component of Australia's sclerophyll (hard-leaved) flora, seven of the genera are restricted to the Wet Tropics. At least three of these, *Placospermum, Sphalmium* and *Carnarvonia* are considered primitive. *Placospermum coriaceum* has the greatest array of primitive features of any living proteaceous genus. It occurs at higher altitudes in the northern part of the Wet Tropics, including Mt Bellenden Ker, Carbine Tableland, Mt Windsor Tableland and Big Tableland.

In fact, the Wet Tropics World Heritage Area plays a vital role in the conservation of the Australian members of the Proteaceae. At least 13 genera (some of which are still to be described) out of a world total of 76 occur in the Wet Tropics and 40 species are restricted to the area.

The important Casuarinaceae family which has its centre of diversity in Australia, occupies habitats ranging from beaches to arid regions, with one genus occurring in rainforest. Fossil evidence indicates that the ancestral form was the East Gondwanan rainforest genus *Gymnostoma,* which was widespread in Australia around 50 to 60 million years ago. *Gymnostoma* now has a relict distribution in Australia with just one species surviving, *Gymnostoma australianum,* which is restricted to the Roaring Meg–Alexandra Creek valleys.

The Wet Tropics flora

Within the Wet Tropics, there are more than 3000 species of vascular plants, representing 1164 genera and 210 families. Of the genera, 75 are found only in Australia and 43 are restricted to the Wet Tropics.

Another palm dominated vineforest is that formed by the fan palm *Licuala ramsayi*. These forests are relatively uncommon, forming in very wet areas of the lowlands and foothills on soils formed from schists and granites with seasonally impeded drainage. Only small patches have survived such as the Tully-Mission Beach area and here at Hutchinson Creek between the Daintree and Bloomfield Rivers.   P. LIK

More than 700 species are found only in this area.

Many examples of isolated populations of tree species occur throughout the rainforests of the World Heritage Area, both on the lowlands and in the uplands. Species included on the lowlands are *Storkiella australiensis* and *Noahdendron nicholasii* which are restricted to near Cape Tribulation; *Idiospermum australiense* and *Lindsayomyrtus brachyandrus* have a disjunct distribution between the Cape Tribulation area and the Harveys Creek–Russell River area south of Cairns, both very wet humid tropical lowland areas. On the uplands *Sphalmium racemosum* and *Stenocarpus davalloides* have populations restricted to the Mt Carbine Tableland in the northern section of the World Heritage Area, whereas *Lomatia fraxinifolia*, *Darlingia darlingiana* and *Cardwellia sublimis* are widespread. Much is yet unknown of the species distribution patterns in these rainforests.

The area has a rich orchid flora. Of some 90 species present, about 59 have a restricted distribution with 43 having an extremely small range. *Dendrobium fleckeri*, *D. adae*, *D. carrii* with its creeping rhizome, *Bulbophyllum boonjie* and *Saccolabiopsis rectifolia* are a few examples of the restricted epiphytic orchids. Terrestrial orchids are also represented in the area. The endemic Jewel Orchid, *Anoectochilus yatesiae*, is only found in the darkest, dense upland rainforests of this region. Among the spectacular plants of the Wet Tropics is the Resurrection Plant, *Borya septentrionalis*, which occurs on mountain tops between Mt Pieter Botte and the Cardwell Range. In the drier season, the leaves dry out to a brilliant orange, then rusty brown, but at the onset of the wet season, they turn vivid green overnight.

The origin of seed plants over 320 million years ago was one of the most significant events in the evolution of terrestrial vegetation, an adaptive breakthrough that allowed colonization of habitats that were inhospitable to spore-producing plants and triggered a Lower Carboniferous diversification of vascular plants. This event also significantly facilitated the evolutionary radiation of other terrestrial organisms. The cone-bearing Cycads and Southern Conifers are the most ancient of living seed plants, little changed from ancestors that flourished in the Jurassic Period, termed the 'Age of the Conifers and Cycads' between 136 and 195 million years ago. The flora of this Period was a cosmopolitan flora of conifers, cycads, ferns, seed-ferns, ginkgos, herbaceous lycopods and horsetails. Jurassic fossils from the Talbragar Fish Beds near Gulgong in New South Wales reveal forests comprising *Agathis* and *Podocarpus* conifers with an understorey of the Cycadophyte, *Pentoxylon australica*. The closest modern counterpart of these forests occurs in the World Heritage area with a rare assemblage of the kauri pines, *Agathis robusta* and *Podocarpus grayae*, and the cycad, *Lepidozamia hopei*.

The majestic Kauri Pine (*Agathis robusta)*, which occurs only in the Wet Tropics and on another World Heritage site, Fraser Island which lies about 1000 kilometres south, can be seen at Lake Barrine. The ancient conifers, Hoop Pine (*Araucaria cunninghamii*) and Bunya Pine (*Araucaria bidwillii*) also occur in the Wet Tropics.

The Wet Tropics World Heritage area is a major centre of survival for the cycads. Ten genera and 121 species in three families of cycads are all that remain of a group that has been in existence relatively unchanged for at least 200 million years with the majority of species now considered as rare and threatened. Two of the three cycad families (Cycadaceae, Zamiaceae) and three genera (*Cycas, Lepidozamia, Bowenia*) occur in the Wet Tropics area representing the highest diversity of cycad genera in Australia and the greatest diversity of major cycad groups anywhere in the world.

Lepidozamia hopei, one of the largest cycads in the world, may grow to a height of about 20 metres. Its population today is scattered and disjunct, being found in areas such as the Malbon Thompson

Range. The small fern-like cycad, *Bowenia spectabilis*, one of the smallest in the world, is common in the understorey of rainforest-associated communities. The related *B. serrulata* is represented in the World Heritage Area by small disjunct populations usually associated with Kauri Pines.

Cycads as a group are thought to have originated in the East Gondwanan sector of Pangaea prior to its breakup. The cycads contain more primitive features than any other living group of gymnosperms. Cycads are the only gymnosperm known to fix nitrogen from the atmosphere which is achieved through a symbiotic relationship with blue-green algae in specialized root structure called corraloid roots. The production of motile sperm cells is unique to cycads and one other gymnosperm, *Gingko biloba*. The discovery of this feature in 1896 was hailed as one of the most exciting botanical discoveries of all time, since it provided the missing link between gymnosperms and the ferns and fern allies. The pollination syndrome of cycads involving primitive groups of insect vectors is believed to represent the most primitive pollination system known and the earliest examples of insect–plant symbiosis. The insect vectors involve ancestral beetle families such as Curculionidae (weevils) and Tenebriondae (tenebrionid beetles), Languriidae, Anthribidae (mortar and carpenter bees), Boganiidae and Nitidulidae. *Cycas media*, which occurs on the eastern coast of Queensland including the Wet Tropics and in New Guinea, is pollinated by native bees from the genus *Trigona*.

The Wet Tropics also has the highest diversity of ferns in Australia and one of the highest levels of genetic diversity in the world. Thirty-one (86 per cent) of the 36 known families and 111 of the 364 described genera (30 per cent) of pteridophytes occur in the Wet Tropics. The Wet Tropics contains 64 per cent of species and 88 per cent of the genera of ferns occurring in Australia. Of more than 240 species occurring in these rainforests, 46 are entirely restricted to the area. Some 17 species have extremely restricted distributions within the area. Of the five fern genera that are endemic to Australia, four occur in the Wet Tropics (*Coveniella, Neurosoria, Pteridoblechnum* and *Platyzoma*). *Pteridoblechnum* is the only endemic fern genus restricted to the tropical area of North-east Australia and is represented by *P. acuminatum* at Mt Spurgeon and Mossman Gorge and the widely distributed *P. neglectum*. The Wet Tropics is also well-known for the variety of Tassell Ferns (*Lycopodium* species) growing on tree trunks and rocks.

MOSSMAN

DAINTREE

OTHER PLACES

MOSSMAN/DAINTREE

THE TERRITORY OF THE KUKU YALANJI EXTENDED FROM Cooktown to Mossman and west to the Palmer River. Prominent peaks such as Kalcajagga (Black Mountain), Wundu (Thornton Peak) and Ngalba Bulal (Mt Pieter Botte) had mythical significance for the people. The Daintree and Bloomfield Rivers were, and still are, home of the 'yero' or Rainbow Serpent with the massive boulders in the headwaters being the eggs that it laid. The Kuku Yalanji were coastal traders who regularly visited the Goonganjie people at Cape Grafton to exchange hardwood spears for cane baskets.

Today many of the descendants of the Kuku Yalanji, who had been moved from their traditional lands to missions in earlier times, live at Mossman Gorge or at Wujal Wujal on the Bloomfield River. Here they keep their traditions alive within the framework of modern society and elders guard the Dreamtime stories which infuse the land-scape with a rationale and meaning that comes from knowledge derived from an ancestry stretching thousands of years.

The first recorded European history in the north was by James Cook whose journey came to a halt when his ship struck a reef in 1770. Cape Tribulation was named for his troubles and after freeing the ship and limping further north to present-day Cooktown, he was to spend time there having the ship repaired and making forays into the hinterland with his botanist Joseph Banks.

The discovery of gold in 1873 on the Palmer River, north-west of Cooktown, brought thousands of European and Asian prospectors to the region. The adventurer Christie Palmerston fossicked and spent periods exploring the McLeod, Daintree and Bloomfield River dis-tricts. For the next 15 years he was to play a leading role in further gold and land exploration. Although he always travelled with an Aboriginal guide, his Upper Daintree journals record accounts of his skirmishes with Aborigines of 'unconquerable hostility'. He chose a campsite clearing in the rainforest, called 'Jungur' by the local people, from where he followed Aboriginal pathways in search of gold and tin on his prospecting expeditions.

While Palmerston found some gold, others were not so lucky. Local names such as Grogan's Folly and Graveyard Gully attest to the hardship endured by most of the newcomers who faced enormous odds to make a living in the harsh terrain.

Agricultural settlement in the Daintree was underway by the

1880s with a variety of enterprises including tropical fruits and sugar cane, a crop which eventually failed because of the distance from the nearest mill. A small steamship brought provisions to the riverside town of Daintree, except at the height of the Wet Season when the normally placid river became a torrent. The writer Ion Idriess, who spent time prospecting around the Bloomfield River early in this century, wrote one of the best accounts of the wet season, that time of the year when heavy rain makes the going tough:

> A week of unceasing tropical rain came until everything looked so like rain that there seemed to be no air, just one soft hissing and the wet smell of vegetation and earth. The jungle was so misty that we could not see past the trees encircling the clearing. The swollen creek hurried past high over the moss of usually dry boulders, crashing over rocky bars to fall in a wind-blown boom into the gorge, thence over fall after fall on its way to the Distant Daintree. The Singing Creek came tumbling over rock and fern and palm-tree root, singing as ever through its lullaby was now an orchestra. Water was welling along every branch, pouring down every tree-trunk dripping from every leaf; the lawyer-canes gleamed like the broad leaves of the water plants. The cat-bird was silent.

At the turn of the century, Port Douglas was the major northern port because of its proximity to the goldfields. A rival to Cairns, the dominance of the town was threatened when the Cairns–Kuranda railway opened in 1891 and shattered in 1911 when a cyclone destroyed much of the town.

Today, travelling north from Cairns is a scenic journey with the ocean almost lapping at the highway in several places. After skirting the

This is a sociable occasion for two pairs of Dainty Tree Frog *(Litoria gracilenta)*. Here they are shown grappling in a prelude to breeding known as 'amplexus'. Groups of these animals congregate around temporary pools and along creeks swollen by the rains of the Wet Season to call for mates and to breed. M. TRENERRY

MacAlister Range for a way, cane fields come back into view before a turn-off to the right leads to Port Douglas. This once sleepy little town, now becoming a major tourism destination, is a stepping-off point for trips to rainforests and the reefs. Back on the highway, about 20 mins drive further north, is the sugar town of Mossman.

Daintree National Park, Mossman Gorge

Covering the eastern slopes of the Mount Carbine Tableland, the northern edge of Windsor Tableland and the valley in between, this section of Daintree NP is a largely inaccessible, mountainous area which includes the catchment for the Daintree and Mossman Rivers. By travelling 5 km west from Mossman you come to the only part of the southern section of the park which can be easily visited – the popular Mossman Gorge. Although bushwalking in other parts of the park is permitted, it is recommended only for those who are fit and experienced walkers. Permits are required for overnight bush camping and safety forms must be completed before embarking. For these, and other advice, contact the QDEH office in Mossman.

Mossman Gorge caters well for its visitors and is one of the best places in the Wet Tropics to get an introduction to rainforests. For this reason it is one of the most visited areas and if you are looking to avoid crowds try to plan your visit for times other than in the middle of the day when buses are likely to pull in. Allow at least an hour-and-a-half for the visit. Toilets and picnic facilities are provided here, but camping is not permitted. It is a great spot to be on a hot day. While it is popular as a swimming spot, swimmers should be aware that several drownings have occurred here due to submerged rocks and strong currents can be experienced after heavy rains.

The gorge, carved out of the granite mountain range by the Mossman River on its rapid descent from the tableland, is dominated by the rock-faced peak Wurrumbu or, as it is otherwise known, the Bluff. The area is an example of lowland tropical rainforest. On the rainforest circuit walk you may notice how the trees, shrubs and vines vary with the change in topography. More than 100 species have been identified and some of them have been labelled for easy identification. As well, the Aboriginal heritage is recognised with signs which explain some of the Kuku Yalanji peoples' uses of this forest. An excellent

There is considerable variation within extensive tracts of rainforest. Along the reaches of this stream at Mossman Gorge a special community of rheophytes or water-loving plants predominate. These include the Water Gum (*Tristaniopsis exiliflora*) with its gnarled and water-worn roots exposed, the magnificent Golden Penda (*Xanthostemon chrysanthus*) and River Cherries (*Syzygium tierneyanum*). PETER LIK

Large and often intricately contorted woody flanges which develop at the base of the trunks of several species of rainforest tree are known as buttresses. These are structures which appear to be related to soil factors and possibly function to brace the trees in unconsolidated substrates or to facilitate root aeration and/or nutrient uptake.   R. RITCHIE

plant guide booklet, with over 50 named tree species, is available from the QDEH office in Mossman.

From the carpark there are two paths with steps leading to a suspension bridge across Rex Creek. From here begins a 2.7 km circuit track which is easy walking.

You will soon come to a lookout with a view of the peak called Manjal Dimbi by the Kuku Yalanji, which, roughly translated, means 'mountain holding back'. The large humanoid rock represents Kubirri who came to the aid of the people when they were persecuted by an evil spirit Wurrumbu. Kubirri holds back the evil spirit which is now confined to the upper Mossman River. Just past the lookout the track branches into a loop. To begin the circuit take the left fork.

As you continue along a ridge, there are views into a creek and a massive fig tree with a seat nearby. Look just past here for more smaller figs which are in the process of strangling their host trees. The walk passes through a sawn opening of a fallen tree.

After about half-an-hour's walk, take a branch track which leads off to the left to a tributary of Wurrumbu Creek, just 100 m from the main trail. This typical little mountain stream is the epitome of rainforest scenery.

Just before you rejoin the track, notice the massively spreading fig tree roots which run along the ground. Near the end of the walk look for another fig with its flying buttresses. You will soon hear the sound of the Mossman River which indicates the end of the trail is near. Retrace your steps, taking time to view the creek with its massive boulders as you walk back to the carpark

Mossman to Daintree River

Twenty-five kms north of Mossman is the turn-off to the right which leads to the Daintree River ferry and the Cape Tribulation Road. By staying on the road, you may travel the 11 km past a Butterfly Farm to the small town of Daintree. The ferry operates from 6.00 am to 12.00 midnight year-round with the exception of Christmas Day and Easter Sunday. Just before the ferry there is a small wharf where a river cruise departs while at the southern ferry terminus is a cafe and a Wet Tropics information centre.

Be warned, that from May to November, you will be sure to experience a 'mega' tourist situation from here on. All the attention that was focused on the area over road-building and logging activities in the 1980s has ensured its popularity. The amount of traffic on the roads makes for a less than satisfying 'wilderness' experience for the day tourist. The rush to get up and back in a day from Cairns means that tour operators take clients to a string of well-worn tracks and facilities and people are given very little time to understand fully the intricacies of the rainforest and its surrounds.

It is worth noting that there are many other places in the Wet Tropics where you can experience the rainforests without having to

Green Tree Ants are ever-present, hard working creatures which fuse leaves to form large colonial nests in the canopies of tropical forest trees. They play important refuse collection roles and contribute to the cycling of plant nutrients. They also have special relationships with some of the plants in which they live by driving away potential predators.   M. PROCIV

The Marrdja Boardwalk provides easy access to two types of forest. It takes visitors through some imposing complex mesophyll vineforest, sections of which are dominated by feather palms, including the Black Palm (*Normanbya normanbyi*), and fan palms, and into the fringing tall mangrove communities along Oliver Creek. P. LIK

join a 'conga-line' of people down crowded walk-ways. Fortunately the Daintree Rescue Program has been launched in an attempt to solve the dilemmas posed by conflicting land uses. The traffic problem could easily be solved by instituting a park-and-ride facility just across the Daintree River and having a regular bus service running to Cape Tribulation and return with ample stops along the way.

Across the Daintree River

Now that the road is nearly all sealed, the trip to Cape Tribulation is easily undertaken in an ordinary vehicle. And the range of accommodation available, including campsites, allows the possibility of an overnight stay to enjoy the sights of the district at a calm pace.

After about 15 mins drive from the ferry, including the winding road up the range, you come to Alexandra Lookout, a well-developed viewing area looking out over the estuary of the Daintree River. As the road continues you will note that there are many signs warning of the Estuarine Crocodiles that make their home in many of the creeks in the Daintree/Bloomfield area, so be aware if you get too far off the beaten track. It is also sometimes difficult to tell whether you are in a national park or on private property because of the mosaic of land ownership in this area.

The next major turn to the right runs for 6 km to Cow Bay, past the popular Crocodylus Youth Hostel. On the way you pass much subdivision development which was the result of bad planning decisions in the past. Roads lead off to small lots, some of which have been cleared of their ecologically important vegetation. Fortunately, many landowners have chosen not to develop their blocks and authorities are keen to cooperate with landholders and buy back certain areas to include in the national park. At Cow Bay there is a beautiful beach with limited picnic facilities, but no camping is permitted.

There are private camping facilities at Cape Kimberley just across the Daintree River, Cow Bay, Myall Creek and at Cape Tribulation. An excellent National Park camping area with toilets, water and a shower is found at Noah Beach. Wood fires are not permitted and payment is by the self-registration permit system. At Thornton Beach there are day-use facilities. Hostels and other accommodation ranging from basic to luxury are all available in the area.

Daintree National Park, Cape Tribulation Section

Thornton Peak (1375 m), which dominates this national park, has an annual rainfall estimated to be as high as 6000 mm and is most often shrouded in cloud. The vegetation in the summit regions is simple microphyll vine-fern forest and simple microphyll vine-fern thicket. While the rainfall drops to an average of 3850 mm on the coast, there

King Parrot
Alisteris scapularis

More often spotted in a clearing, this bird spends much of its time in the rainforest high in the canopy. Males have the brightest plumage and lead the female in a ritual courting which includes feather ruffling, wing flicking and special calls. The female moves her head from side to side and is rewarded with a ritual feeding.

The female nests in a tree hollow and sits on from three to five eggs for 20 days with her mate bringing a supply of food. The range of food includes seeds, fruit, leaf buds and blossoms. King Parrots will move from the colder tablelands in the winter to lower elevations and return again for the summer.

C. & D. FRITH/FRITHFOTO

is still luxuriant vegetation including unique species of immense scientific importance. Over three-quarters of the Wet Tropics endemic vertebrate species are found here. As a key refuge area for many plant and animal species it is regarded as an epicentre of evolution.

Birds that make their habitat here include Mountain Thornbill, Golden Bowerbird, Tooth-billed Catbird, Bridled Honeyeater, Victoria's Riflebird, and the Pied Monarch. Mammals include Green Ringtail Possum, Spotted-tailed Quoll, Musky Rat-kangaroo, Long-tailed Pigmy-possum and Bennett's Tree-kangaroo. Reptiles include Thornton Peak Skink, Boyd's Forest Dragon and Grey-tailed Skink.

Marrdja Walk

At Oliver Creek, 28 km from the ferry, the Marrdja Walk is an 800 m pathway and boardwalk through a complex lowland rainforest which leads to a mangrove forest. Marrdja is the Kuku Yalanji word for 'rainforest'. Many of the trees are marked and there are good interpretive signs along the way. A short loop path with labelled plants allows you to view more of the forest. The boardwalk leading through the mangroves is especially interesting because this habitat is always difficult to visit and needs to be appreciated for its ecological importance. At the end walkers are rewarded with a great view over the water where Oliver and Noah Creeks' flow to the sea. Allow at least three-quarters of an hour for the walk.

Noah Creek and its tributaries are lowland refugial forests and are major sites of endemism, representing some of the world's most significant centres of survival of families of angiosperms originating in Gondwana. Some species are central to the total evolutionary development of flowering plants. The diggings on the forest floor have more than likely been caused by feral pigs which are a major problem throughout the Wet Tropics. Some, however, may be the results of the work of those voracious foragers the Orange-footed Scrubfowl *(Megapodius reinwardt)*.

Cape Tribulation Walk

At the settlement of Cape Tribulation, look for the short side road to the right just before Jungle Village and opposite the store. This leads to a small carpark where a short boardwalk leads through mangroves to Myall Beach. From here it is possible to walk north along the beach (preferably at low tide) for about 1.5 km where a track leads off to the

An aerial view looking south from Cowie Beach to a spur of Mount Donovan – a section of the northern Wet Tropics coast where rainforest meets the fringing reef and the two World Heritage Areas abut. This is an area where rainforest is rapidly expanding due to the cessation of the burning practices of Aboriginal people. P. LIK

Tree ferns are another distinctive life form which characterises the moist forests. Here, in Daintree National Park, an almost single-species stand of *Cyathea cooperi* has developed in the full sun of a canopy gap. P. LIK

left to cross the isthmus of the Cape, through rainforest, to the picnic area and carpark. A branch track to the right, Goolkee Track, leads 400 m via a concrete path and elevated boardwalk to a viewing platform overlooking the ocean and the beach and, depending on the weather, allowing a view of the mountain range.

Back along the track, before the carpark, access to the beach is possible. To return to your car you have the choice of retracing your steps or walking back along the main road. Of course, you could begin the walk from the Cape Tribulation car park and follow the directions in reverse.

It is possible to walk from Myall Beach north to Emmagen Creek. This 4-hour return walk is best attempted with an outgoing tide.

North of Cape Tribulation

Easily accessible from Cooktown are the two northernmost national parks in the Wet Tropics, Black Mountain National Park and Cedar Bay National Park. To avoid the virtually untrafficable road north of Cape Tribulation, access from the south is best gained via the Peninsula Developmental Road.

This 225 km diversion takes you west of the Great Dividing Range through Mount Molloy, Mount Carbine and Lakeland to Black Mountain NP with its scenic large black granitic tors. A further 20 km to the south is the boundary of Cedar Bay NP. Both parks are undeveloped.

OTHER PLACES TO VISIT

The Rainforest Habitat, Port Douglas

Located just at the turn-off to Port Douglas on the Cook Highway 61 km north of Cairns, this man-made environment for birds and animals is actually an interactive zoo. Created on what used to be a cane farm, it is divided into sections with an enclosed walk-through aviary housing over 60 species of native birds as the main attraction. The vegetation is a mixture of native and introduced species. A few kangaroos and wallabies lie about on a grassed area while some Estuarine Crocodiles bask in enclosures. As well, a small shelter offers close-hand viewing of koalas.

Open from 8.00 am to 5.00 pm daily, the cost of admission is $14 for adults and $7 for children. For double the admission price you get a buffet 'breakfast with the birds' which is literally the case as the restaurant is part of a bird enclosure. If you wish to see a variety of birds at close quarters, then this is the place for you, especially at feeding time which is 9.30 am. Alternatively, you may wish to try your luck with binoculars and a good identification book in one of the Wet Tropics' natural areas.

Daintree River Cruises

Departing from the southern side of the Daintree River crossing it is possible to view the rainforests from the comfort of the 'River Train', in linked punt 'carriages', where you get a running commentary on points of interest, which may include Estuarine Crocodiles, a fruit bat colony, White-bellied Sea-eagles *(Halilltus chryogaster)* or waders. A boardwalk mangrove and rainforest walk and morning or afternoon tea are also included. Prices range from $12 for an early morning one-hour cruise to $22 for the two-and-a-half hour trip, with children 4–14 half price.

Daintree Environment Centre

About 10 km north of the ferry, on the right, is a turn-off to the Daintree Environment Centre. This privately owned and operated centre provides a good introduction to rainforests. The Centre, surrounded by rainforest, features a short self-guided walk on a raised boardwalk, an informative visitor centre with a display area and a small theatre with videos of rainforest topics. Admission charges are $8 and $6 concession.

Wonga
Snapper Island
Daintree (Dagmar Range) National Park

DAINTREE NATIONAL PARK

Mt Spurgeon
Mossman
Miallo

Dayman Point (Rocky Point)

Mt Demi

MOSSMAN
Palm Beach
Newell
Mossman Gorge
Cooya Beach
South Mossman

Lyons

Low Isles

PORT DOUGLAS
Cruises Shell Display
Resort
Rainforest Habitat

Sisters Reef

Tonue Reef

Batt Reef

Mt Lewis
Rumula

Mt Frazer
Julatten

Yule Point
Oak Beach

MARLIN

WARNING
Swimming in coastal waters in summer
can be dangerous due to marine stingers.
Always seek local advice.

Mount Molloy

Rex Lookout
White Cliff Point
Hartleys Creek Crocodile Farm

Black Mountain

COAST

Mt Danbulan

Red Cliff Point

Ellis Beach
Double Island

Lake Mitchell

Koah

①

Palm Cove *Wildworld Wildlife Park*
Clifton Beach
Kewarra Beach
Trinity Beach

Michaelmas

Michaelm National

⑨ ⑩ Kuranda
Resort
Scenic Railway

Oyster Reef
Upolu Reef
Upolu Cay
National Park

Biboohra

②
Yorkeys Knob

Barron Falls
Smithfield Heights
Lake Placid

Skyrail

Holloways Beach
Machans Beach

Arlin Re

MAREEBA
Trainland

③
Barron Falls Gorge
National Park
Redlynch

Green Island
Green Island National Park

⑧

Davies Creek
National Park
Falls

Bare Hill
Crystal Cascades

⑥ ⑤
CAIRNS

Cape Grafton

Lake Morris

Mt Tiptree
④

Glen
Boughton
White Rock

Yarrabah

Walkamin

Edmonton
Sugarworld

May Peak

Resort
Fitzroy Island
Fitzroy Island
National Park

⑦

Tinaroo Falls

Kamma
Grey Peaks
National Park

Never swim in rivers and streams
where you see this sign.
Crocodiles may be present.
Always seek local advice.

Tolga
Kairi

Kauri Creek
Orchid Farm
Lake Euramoo
Mobo Crater
Cathedral Fig

Steam Train Tours
Gordonvale

Aloomba

Lake Tinaroo

Little
Mulgrave
Walshes
Pyramid

ATHERTON
Yungaburra

Fishery Falls
Mt Massey

Palmer Point
High Island

**FRANKLIN
ISLANDS
NATIONAL
PARK**

Curtain Fig

Heales Lookout
Lake Barrine
Crater Lakes Nat Pk
Lake Eacham
Goldsborough
Valley

River cruises
Kearneys Falls
Deeral

Mutchero Inlet
National Park
Mutchero Inlet

Normanby Island

Falls
Malanda

North
Johnstone

Bellenden Ker

Bellenden Ker
Russell Island

Hillview

WOOROONOORAN

Russell
River
National
Park

**GRAHAM RANGE
NATIONAL PARK**

Butchers Creek

Tarzali

(BELLENDEN KER)

The Boulders

Lamins Hill Lookout
Topaz

NATIONAL

Mt Bartle Frere
Queensland's tallest
peak 1622 metres

Wyvuri Swamp

Milla Milla
Falls

Zillie Falls

PARK

Bramston Beach

Minga
Millaa
Elinjaa Falls

Josephine Falls

Miriwinni
Babinda

Kilometres
0 5 10 15

KURANDA

Barron Gorge National Park ①
Wrights Lookout ②

CAIRNS

Lake Placid and Stoney Creek ③
Crystal Cascades and Lake Morris ④
Mt Whitfield Conservation Park ⑤

OTHER PLACES

Flecker Botanic Gardens, Cairns ⑥
Fitzroy Island ⑦
Green Island National Park ⑧
Jumrum Creek Conservation Park ⑨
Rainforestation, Kuranda ⑩

KURANDA/CAIRNS

LOCAL HISTORIAN EDWINA TOOHEY WRITES EVOCATIVELY OF THE first people living in the present-day Cairns region:

From the Barron Gorge down to its delta was the territory of the Djabuganydji. These were very much river people, cruising up and down the Barron and its feeder streams in their rafts and cedar canoes, spearing fish and trapping turtles and Estuarine Crocodiles. On simple bark or dug-out canoes they paddled up the Barron River to trade with neighbouring Tableland groups – a trade in spear-throwers, bamboo spears and nautilus shell. In their outriggers they headed out to sea as far as their kinspeople at Port Douglas to conduct trade or to hunt and harpoon turtles and dugong. From the sea, not the river, came the greatest prize of all, the nautilus shell, with its beautiful reflective colours linked inseparably to Gudju-gadju, the powerful Rainbow Serpent, and its healing powers.

It was from the Bulurru (plant) ancestors of the Djabuganydji that the knowledge necessary for survival came: how to set a trap for turkeys under the walnut tree, how to spread the sticky sap of the strangler fig on tree branches to trap birds and how to crack the toughest of tree nuts, the Kuranda Quandong. Within their territory, bounded by the Barron River and the sea and stretching for many kilometres, was a plentiful food source that could be tapped using raw materials available from the river, the reef and the forests. Fish were snared by woven fibre nets slung across the river or swept downstream with the currents into stone fish traps and eels were enticed into baskets made from lawyer cane. These forests also provided the Djabuganydji with a seasonal harvest of edible shoots from wild ginger and calamus vine, the bitter-sweet fruit of the quandong, wild raspberries, plums, cherries and seed pods of the yellow walnut, black pine and candlenut trees.

Cairns

Established at the head of Trinity Inlet, the beginnings of Cairns were as a sea port in competition with Port Douglas to the north. The Barron River was the fluid highway down which logs were floated to Cairns for milling from where they were sent south to market.

As the forests were exhausted new settlers put the valuable land under a variety of crops, including sugar cane. Late last century farmers were also growing rice, while tobacco and cotton were experimented along with cocoa and coffee. As an early writer on the Cairns region noted:

Still one of the top attractions for visitors to far north Queensland, the Kuranda train continues to take daytrippers on the picturesque journey from Cairns to Kuranda, over one-hundred years after the line was first constructed.   P. LIK

On every side of it the rich alluvial deposits washed down from the mountains maintain a florid vegetation. Dense jungly scrubs present a tangled wealth of tropic flora; ferns, orchids, and flowering plants clothe the soil, above them wave the broad leaves of the wild banana, while over all tower graceful palms, and mighty cedars of vast girth invite the axe of the timber-getter.

Around the turn of last century the artist Ellis Rowan was travelling to 'the depths of jungles' and to 'wild mountain districts' in search of specimens to depict. She specialised in watercolour studies of flowering plants. Rowan travelled widely, and unusually for that time, often independently, throughout Australia and New Zealand including the rainforests of north Queensland. The forests near Myola on the Barron River she wrote, had a 'network of branches above all hung and festooned with thickets of clematis, convolvulus, and flowering begonias, erythrinas, tossing acacias, feathery palms'. The riverbanks were 'green with sedges and tall white lilies, and beyond…masses of great moss-grown rocks, and the river tosses and tumbles round and over them, falling in countless cascades into the deep, dark pools below'.

Today, Cairns is a vibrant regional city, struggling to expand to meet the demands of the increasing numbers of visitors while at the same time trying to retain its tropical charm. On the streets are a mixture of people including both black and white Australians along with people from Asia, Europe and North America.

The tropical vegetation and northern architecture combine to make this destination unique in Australia, perhaps rivalled only by

Tropical timbers were used for a variety of purposes. Here timberworkers saw a log into sections for splitting into shingles. Before the widespread use of roofing iron, shingle roofs provided a cheap, if labourious, alternative material.

Darwin. While the exclusive boutiques and 'brand name' shops are creeping down the main street, there are night markets which add a touch of alternative lifestyle to the city. And the popularity of the region with backpackers brings a down-to-earth, energetic feeling which adds to the cultural diversity.

Kuranda

Kuranda became a popular resort and day-trip town with the Barron Falls as the major attraction after the Cairns–Kuranda railway was completed in 1891. In fact, it remained the only direct access route until the 1940s when the road up the range was completed.

In 1903 Frederick Dodd arrived and assembled a world-famous insect collection which he displayed, toured and from which he sent specimens to international collectors. A great promoter of Kuranda, he was quick to counter the impression that summer was not a good time for visiting the tropical north:

> Summer! when the gigantic and often weeping cloud-masses grandly roll across the blue, so very blue, sky; when the branching and often violet lightning flashes out and the deep thunder reverberates

The waters of Stoney Creek tumble over a more resistant mass of metamorphic rocks from the Hodgkinson Formation in Barron Gorge National Park. Steep gradients are a feature of short easterly flowing streams draining the Great Dividing Range.　　　　　P. LIK

through the hills and valleys; when the water gushes from our roofs and freely drips from every leaf; when the swift-winged metallic starling darts over and through the scrubs...the time when the fireflies glitter and the joyous cicada sings all through the day.

In 1935 the enormous power of the Barron River was harnessed for hydro-electric power when a station was constructed at Barron Gorge. Like many scenic small towns, tourism became important to the local economy after timber-getting and marginal farming activities went into decline. The past 20 years have seen Kuranda and the surrounding district become a popular residential area – virtually mountain suburbs of Cairns.

The town is rapidly falling victim to its own popularity and at the height of the tourist season it is a hive of activity. The Kuranda Markets, held on Wednesday, Thursday, Friday and Sunday, are the busiest days. Other attractions include the Tjapukai Aboriginal Dance Theatre, the Butterfly Sanctuary and the Noctarium.

One of the best ways to get here from Cairns is to take the train. In the one-and-a-half hour journey you pass through 15 tunnels, go around 98 panoramic curves and past breathtaking waterfalls for the 34 km to the Kuranda railway station. On the way you get to look out over the countryside and to also appreciate the engineering feat and the perseverance of the people who built this railway. From the station, famous for its profusion of potted plants, it is only a short walk to a number of attractions.

Another way to get to Kuranda is by taking the newly-built gondola cableway, the Skyrail, which begins from Smithfield just north of Cairns and terminates at Kuranda. Running for 7.5 kms, the half-hour journey takes you over the canopy of the forest and gives great views of the surrounding district. There are two stops on the way: Red Peak, where you change for the final stage and where there is a boardwalk and Barron Falls, where the CSIRO has constructed a rainforest interpretive centre. Controversial as a concept because of its potential ecological and aesthetic impact, the Skyrail is destined to become a major attraction for the region. It is possible to combine both the railway and the cableway and buy a combined ticket to travel one way on each.

Barron Gorge National Park

As 'wilderness' on the edge of Cairns, Barron Gorge National Park is probably one of the most intensely visited national parks in North Queensland. For visitors, the park is essentially divided into two, with the upper section accessible from Kuranda, while the lower section is reached by the Barron Gorge Road off the Redlynch–Smithfield

Rainforests suffer considerable disturbance. Those in the vicinity of Kuranda are no exception with the proliferation of Lawyer Cane or Wait-a-while (*Calamus* spp.) and pioneer species such as the Brown Salwood Wattle (*Acacia aulacocarpa*) reflecting previous cyclone and logging damage.   P. LIK

Road north of Cairns. The Barron River plunges 265 m over Barron Falls though its spectacle and power has been harnessed by a hydro-electric power station. Below the power station rafting companies take advantage of this 'used' water which is discharged so that thrill-seeking visitors enjoy the brief but exciting ride over cascades and small falls, through spectacular rainforested gorge scenery only minutes from the centre of Cairns.

Mammals found within the park include a variety of possums, Lumholtz's Tree-kangaroo *(Dendrolagus lumholtzii)*, Quolls (*Dasyurus* spp.) and a variety of flying foxes (*Pteropus* spp.). Birds include a variety of parrots, Brush-turkeys, Noisy Pittas *(Pitta versicolor)* and, in some places, the Cassowary *(Casuarius casuarius)*. For further information on this park contact the QDEH office in Cairns.

Barron Falls Lookout

No secret destination this one, for over 100 years visitors have made the journey to this scenic spot. Day-trippers come to the mountains from hot Cairns to picnic, walk in the cool forests and enjoy the views. About 3 km from Kuranda along the Barron Falls Road you reach the well signposted Barron Falls Lookout. Recently upgraded picnic facilities and a lookout over the spectacular chasm are the attractions while

a graded 120 m walk will take you down to the Barron Falls Railway Station (be careful to watch out for trains!) and provide a better view over the falls.

This is a great vantage point whether the falls are flowing or not. In the Wet Season, or after a recent deluge, the sight is awesome with the thunderous roar almost drowning out speech and swirling mists and spray, even at the rail station, making photography a challenge. At other times of the year the Falls are 'turned on' at the hydro station at various times for visitors to observe. An old track beyond the Falls is dangerous and should not be attempted.

Wrights Lookout and beyond

A further 1 km beyond the Barron Falls Lookout is Wrights Lookout. Another easily accessible good vantage point, this time a view down the gorge, over canefields and out to sea. Waterfalls can be seen and heard tumbling out of the rainforest and falling to the river below. A number of walks may be taken from this point.

From behind the lookout, a locked access gate marks the entry to the National Park and bars vehicular entry to a road that runs along the gorge, above the rail line, to service electricity towers and for fire management purposes. This 20 min picturesque walk, particularly so early in the morning, goes through moss- and fern-covered cypress, eucalypt and casuarina forest to Surprise Creek. This creek is a pleasant enough destination in itself, however, once there you have a number of alternatives.

The road continues on out of the forest for about a 1 hour walk providing many views along the way to where it terminates at Red Bluff where the power lines drop steeply to the valley below. Take water with you on this one-way walk.

Back at Surprise Creek good rock-hopping can be had upstream, however, a short rock-hop downstream will bring you to the head of Surprise Creek Falls which is situated immediately below a high-level railway bridge. Enjoy the deep, clear swimming pools here before returning the way you came or follow the graded track that zig-zags down the ridge on the left side of the creek to the Hydro-Electric station below – where your pick-up person is waiting if you're organised.

Walking back along the rail line to Wrights Lookout is not recommended and there are plenty of Queensland Rail signs reminding you of the tenure of the property.

The Barron Gorge is one of the deeply incised river systems within the coastal ranges of the Wet Tropics. Easily accessible from Cairns this area is renown for its water-based activities.   P. CURTIS

Quiet places also exist along the Barron River. Here at Lake Placid visitors can experience the tranquillity and splendour of the forest by travelling by canoe to some of the less well-trodden spots. P. CURTIS

Lake Placid and Stoney Creek

Lake Placid, actually an impoundment of the Barron River created by natural rocky barrages, is one of the many freshwater playgrounds of the locals when the beaches are hazardous due to the presence of marine stingers. Located at the mouth of Barron Gorge it has all the accoutrements of the great family relaxing spot. Deep, clear, fresh water, lushly landscaped picnic areas, barbecues, amenities block and even a kiosk that serves Devonshire Teas. A trail leads you a couple of hundred metres upstream through tall rainforest, past a large Brush-turkey nesting mound to some rocky vantage points. No fishing is allowed but canoeing is permitted.

The drive upstream from Lake Placid takes you deep into Barron Gorge and to the Hydro Electric station. This drive is spectacular and distracting to say the least. In places the road is cut into sheer rock faces and in others waterfalls cascade down next to the road. All this spectacle and splendour and you are virtually in suburban Cairns.

On the other side of Lake Placid, Stoney Creek joins the Barron River. Drive downstream, cross the river at the old bridge and proceed back upstream through the Kamerunga Rainforest Estate to the end of the road where Stoney Creek tumbles down through the forest. A beautiful short walk along an old water pipeline maintenance track follows the stream up past many idyllic pools shaded from the sun by the dense forest canopy.

Crystal Cascades and Copperlode Dam (Lake Morris)

Flowing out of the hills west of Cairns is Freshwater Creek. Its waters have been impounded in a high rainforested valley by Copperlode Dam, forming Lake Morris. The winding 19 km scenic drive up from Reservoir Road in the suburb of Mooroobool provides wonderful views over Cairns and environs before dropping down into the upper Freshwater Creek valley.

The local council has provided some excellent day visitor facilities including picnic tables, gas and wood barbecues, another kiosk for the unprepared and all in lush grassed surroundings with a postcard view over the lake and its spectacular mountain backdrop of the Lamb Range. The facilities are usually stretched to the limit on a hot weekend and during school holidays when it appears as if half of Cairns' population is to be found here. There are some short walks to vantage points around the dam wall and spillway. Swimming, boating and fishing are not permitted.

Lake Morris is the main water supply reservoir for the Cairns area and downstream below the water intake is the popular recreation area of Crystal Cascades. It is 10 km up the valley from the Red Beret

Rainforest trees come in a variety of shapes and sizes. Here, within complex mesophyll vineforest, the buttresses of the Spurwood (*Dysoxylum pettegrewianum*) and the fruit and flower scars of the cauliflorous and aptly-named Bumpy Satinash (*Syzygium cormiflorum*) stand in considerable contrast.   R. RITCHIE

Purple-crowned Pigeon
Ptilinopus superbus

This brightly coloured bird is shy and hard to spot as it feeds high in the canopy on one of over 50 species of fruiting plants. These include Bollywoods, Blue Walnuts and Rusty Laurels. The female lacks many of the colours of the male. Both sexes share the incubation task which takes place in a seemingly frail, simple nest consisting of a bundle of interlocking twigs.

Here the male is minding the nest where a chick has hatched after 14 days of incubation. Purple-crowned pigeons prefer a lowland rainforest habitat although they will migrate to the uplands in the Winter. They range from Yeppoon to Cape York Peninsula.

C. & D. FRITH/FRITHFOTO

Hotel corner at Redlynch, through rapidly developing rural residential suburbs. From the car park at the end of the road it is a 15 min walk past swimming holes to the locked gate near the water intake. This walk could well be the best quick introduction to the Wet Tropics World Heritage Area near Cairns.

This access road to the water intake has been etched into the side of the steep rainforest-clad canyon. Late in the year the bright red fruit of a rainforest pandanus stands out like beacons from the tangle of greenery clinging tenuously to the moist slopes. Public access stops at the locked gate where a usually vandalised small tin sign announces you have arrived at 'Crystal Cascade'. This is almost an anticlimax after passing many pools and cascades on the way up.

A walk from Crystal Cascades to Copperlode Dam is possible and an unmaintained track commences from behind the toilets, just up from the car park and zig-zags up the ridge through a number of forest types. The 50 min walk brings you to the bitumen road about 400 m away from the gates to the Lake Morris picnic area.

Do not succumb to the temptation of walking back down the creek to Crystal Cascades. No track exists and there is rough and difficult terrain to traverse including steep cliff faces and stinging trees to negotiate. To top it off there are some well-built barbed-wire gates near the intake to discourage the curious.

Mt Whitfield Conservation Park

Only ten minutes drive from the centre of the city, this remnant of rainforest, tall open forest and eucalypt woodland with cycads, is surrounded by the burgeoning suburbs of Cairns. Enter the park from Collins Avenue opposite the Gardens. By taking the Blue Arrow Trail, a medium grade 7.5 km loop, it is possible you will encounter one of the 12 cassowaries that have managed to survive in this forest. Because you climb through several hundred metres of elevation you should allow 3 hours for this relatively strenuous walk.

By taking the first two right forks you will come to a lookout with views over the airport, about 1 km from the start. Rejoin the trail turn right and right again and another 250 m takes you to another lookout. From here it is just 150 m to a left fork which will set you on a path for Mt Lumley Hill. About 2.5 km from this fork look for the 400 m side trail on the left to another lookout with its view over the Barron River to the beaches.

The return walk winds down to Hamliffe Creek before continuing up to rejoin the Red Arrow Trail where you may take a right fork and make your way back to Collins Ave.

The shorter 1.5 km loop Red Arrow Trail, which includes the beginning of the other walk, gets you to the first lookout with views over the airport. The return takes you down the headwaters of a small creek back to Collins Ave. For further information contact the QDEH office in Cairns.

OTHER PLACES TO VISIT

Flecker Botanic Gardens

Botanical Gardens fulfil an important function for the propagation, study and preservation of plant species. More and more, these places are becoming custodians of living seed banks and genetic viability. Flecker Botanic Gardens has been expanded over the years to cover 38 ha and is known for its collection of tropical plants which thrive in this warm, moist location. Features of the Gardens include a comprehensive display on the evolution and status of Wet Tropics flora, a fern house, an orchid house, an Aboriginal plant garden and hundreds of named species. Over the road are a collection of pondages known as Centenary Lakes where a raised boardwalk and walking trails lead to a number of botanical delights. It is possible to visit the Mt Whitfield Conservation Park from here also.

Located 4 km north of the centre of Cairns the Gardens are open from 7.30 am to 5.30 pm on weekdays and from 8.30 am on weekends. Admission is free. Follow Sheridan Street north, turn left into

Collins Avenue and 500 m on is the main entrance.

Fitzroy Island National Park
A rainforested island surrounded by coral reef, the beaches are good for swimming and the surrounding waters good for diving. There are several walks including the lighthouse circuit which is an easy two hours. A popular snorkelling destination, Fitzroy Island is well served by a regular ferry service from Cairns. The 20 min Secret Garden rainforest walk starts from behind the Rainforest Restaurant.

Green Island National Park
This coral cay has long been a popular destination, and today is the location of newly developed 5-star resort. At the eastern end of the island a short walk leads through rainforest and it should be possible to see some of the variety of bird life. Green Island is located 27 kms east of Cairns from where a regular fast catamaran service takes 40 mins.

Jumrum Creek Conservation Park
Just outside the boundary of the World Heritage Area, this place could be described as the rainforest in the village, in the village in the rainforest (as promoters describe Kuranda). Jumrum Creek is nevertheless an approximation of what Kuranda once looked like. A walking track of a few hundred metres drops down from Barang Street (parallel and to the east of the main street), crosses the creek at some small cascades and you then have a choice of two short tracks up to join Barron Falls Road.

This Conservation Park suffers the plight of many suburban parks. It is too big to be manicured and well presented (and not in keeping with park management philosophy) and too small to escape the ravages of nearby development and vandalism. The condition of the track is currently not in keeping with its proximity to one of the premier tourist destinations in Australia. Jumrum Creek probably best serves the locals looking for a tranquil walk before or after the tourist inflow arrives, or alternatively, visitors who have arrived by bus, train or Skyrail and who have not yet experienced a tropical rainforest walk.

Some people may find the Kuranda Riverside Walk a better experience. Although substantially more artificial this is a serene walk at any time of the day along the well-grassed south bank of the Barron River below the Railway Station. The tall melaleucas, eucalypts, casuarinas and remnant rainforest species contrast with the densely forested opposite bank with its riot of textured and coloured foliage. There are guided walks and cruises and canoe hire is available.

Rainforestation, Kuranda

Open daily from 9.00 am to 4.00 pm, this popular attraction offers a glimpse of Aboriginal heritage with the Pamagirri Dancers performing in a forest amphitheatre, a Dreamtime Walk which winds up the hill and a rainforest tour in an amphibious army duck. Experienced guides are on hand to explain the Aboriginal uses of the rainforest plants on the 'jungle walk' which is an easy one-hour walk through the rainforest. Admission prices for all the activities are $22 for adults and $11 for children. The Dancers perform twice daily so check for times beforehand.

ATHERTON TABLELAND

Crater Lakes National Park ①
Lake Barrine and Lake Eacham
Mt Hypipamee National Park ②
The Curtain Fig, Yungaburra State Forest ③

Danbulla Forest Drive

Kauri Creek State Forest ④
Lake Euramoo ⑤
Mobo Creek Crater ⑥
The Cathedral Fig ⑦

Tully Gorge National Park ⑧

OTHER PLACES

Malanda ⑨
Wongabel State Forest ⑩
Bromfield Swamp ⑪
Millstream Falls National Park ⑫
Millaa Millaa Waterfall Circuit ⑬

ATHERTON TABLELAND

MT SPEC IN THE SOUTH WAS THE START OF A COASTAL PATHWAY that stretched as far as the Bloomfield River. Another pathway ran from Port Douglas to the Atherton Tableland. As Edwina Toohey writes:

> a track led south past Lake Eacham into the tribal territory of the Mamu people of the Johnstone River valley, and another passed through Russell Pocket to follow the Barron River northwards into the territory of their neighbours to the north, the Yidinyi. Countless mazes of smaller paths invariably led away to different sites, be they regular campsites, bora grounds, painting sites, food trees or even places where the best spear-making sticks could be found.

Sections of some of the trails are still visible today, and many are still being walked by people keen to maintain their traditional knowledge and pass it on to successive generations.

Recent research suggests the rainforests of the Atherton Tableland expanded about 6000 years ago and the people must have adapted their way of life during these changes in vegetation. This correlates with early white observers of this area who noted inhabited clearings of about one-tenth of a hectare, and reported that Aborigines took 'particular care to keep the place free from jungle, which would creep over it in a few seasons if allowed'.

The Tableland was named after the first white settler, John Atherton, who in 1876 drove his cattle from Mt Garnet to select Emerald End, near the present town of Mareeba. Living a precarious existence with his family on the frontier, he lost several hundred cattle a year to hostile Aborigines for the first few years. Atherton also found payable tin at Tinaroo. Later gold discoveries gave Mareeba a brief period of prosperity but by the turn of the century the 'gold' was more likely to be in the form of the valuable timber which was to be found in the rainforests which were falling to the settler's axe.

With the majority of the Tableland's rainforests cleared the remaining sites are very important for both recreation and research. In fact, despite the past disturbance there are six types of rainforest and the area is a major repository of biodiversity. Simple notophyll vine forests are the main forest type on the Tableland at higher elevations (above 800 m) on soils derived from granites, metamorphics and acid volcanics. The fossil pollen record for the Tableland suggests there were several cycles of contraction of rainforest over the past 200,000 years with replacement by araucarian forests and open woodland followed by re-expansion of rainforest. During the last 10,000 years increasing rainfall favoured the expansion of rainforest which restricted the araucarian forests to isolated patches.

Billed as cool, quiet and spectacular, the Tableland is a good antidote to the hustle and bustle of the coastal lowlands. There are a variety of excellent rainforest sites to visit and enough 'must see' places to occupy a couple of days. And with 48 terrestrial endemic vertebrate species, there is also a great chance of sighting wildlife.

Crater Lakes National Park

About 5 km east of Yungaburra on the Gillies Highway is a junction in the road. Travelling 7 km towards Gordonvale will bring you to the turn-off to the right for Lake Barrine. A right turn at the junction and a couple of kms drive will bring you to the turn-off on the left to Lake Eacham. If you are coming from Gordonvale along the Gillies Highway look for the signs on the left once you have ascended the Tableland. Lakes Eacham and Barrine are two of the most impressive of several extinct craters (maars) on the Tableland. The cores, which are now lakes, are the result of an eruption about 10,000 years ago. They are now filled with rainwater.

The Ngadjan story for how the lakes were formed relates closely to the scientific one:

> The camping-place began to twist and crack. While this was happening there was in the sky a red cloud... the people tried to run... but were swallowed by a crack which opened in the ground.

Looking through Stringybark (*Eucalyptus intermedia*) and Turpentine (*Syncarpia glomulifera*) open forest across the cane fields and orchards of the Mulgrave Valley from a vantage point along the Gillies Highway – one of the three major routeways to the Atherton Tableland.   P. LIK

The local Aboriginal legend also asserts that the lakes are linked by an underground tunnel which was home to a tree trunk with the potential to turn into a giant crocodile 'Canyahra'. It is from this beast which may emerge the spirit of Mt Bellenden Ker, 'Murgalainya'. This story is at odds with modern science, however, as the water does not appear to equalise in height between the two lakes.

The Lakes, with their narrow band of protective rainforests, were both declared national parks in 1934 and have just recently been renamed as Crater Lakes NP. They are very similar in origin and appearance, nearly identical in height above sea level (730 m) and both about 65 m deep. At Lake Eacham, however, the water can only escape by seepage or evaporation while at Lake Barrine there are these means, plus it is the headwater for a small creek. For further park enquiries contact the QDEH office at Lake Eacham.

Lake Barrine

Lake Barrine gets more visitors than Lake Eacham because of its well-established facilities which include tea rooms, shops and a Wet Tropics display. Another popular attraction is the 40-minute guided boat tour which traverses the lake.

There is also a 5 km circuit walking trail which enables an easy walk around the lake. It begins from near the teahouse, from where a 900 m track will lead you to the two huge Kauri trees *(Microstachya araucariacea)* which are believed to be over 1000 years old and are about 50 m high. This species is rare and threatened and their geographic distribution is restricted to 100 km from this site. The trees are also a floristic link to the coniferous forests which grew in Australia 300 million years ago. From these forests climatic changes and volcanic upheaval brought about the development of the rainforests and then the eucalypts.

The track continues past the headwater of the small creek which takes water out of the lake in the Wet Season, heads inland for a way and then returns to the banks of the lake which are followed for the rest of the walk. Along the way you pass through a variety of upland rainforest vegetation including Bumpy Satinash which is recognised by its distinctive cream flowers in spring. Look out for Boyd's Forest Dragon and, by the waterside, the impressive but harmless Amethystine Python. Allow 2 hours for the walk.

Lake Eacham

There are excellent facilities for day visitors here including change sheds for swimmers, covered benches, toilets and barbecues. Brush-turkeys make it their business to patrol the open areas, scavenging for a feed of the visitors left-overs. Please don't feed them because they can become depen-dant on visitors who, being a fickle lot, tend to stay away at certain times of the year. There are always less people here than at Lake Barrine and if time is pressing, the walk around the lake is about 2 km shorter.

From near the start of the main lake circuit walk is a 500 m self-guided walk which can be undertaken with the help of a brochure available at either end of the walk. Although the brochure recommends starting from the other end (near the ranger station) it is possible to do the walk in reverse by simply reading the notes in reverse order. Plants to look out for include: Rose Butternut, Red Tulip Oaks, Wild Apples *(Syzygium spp.)* Corkwoods *(Melicope moluccana)* and Candlenuts *(Aleurites moluccana),* while animals include: Musky Rat-kangaroos during the day and Red-legged Pademelons in the evening.

Caught brilliantly by the photographer, this Double-eyed Fig Parrot *(Psittaculirostris diophthalma macleayai)* appears transfixed.

These hard-to-spot birds live among the canopy in pairs or small groups. They are often noticed when falling pieces of fruit draw attention to their otherwise quiet feeding habits. They form a nesting chamber by excavating rotting branches of trees. The female incubates the eggs and both parents feed the chicks. M. TRENERRY

There is also a turtle viewing area nearby, but you are asked not to feed the turtles or the fish you may see here. Commonly seen birds at Lake Eacham include: Grey-headed Robin, Eastern Whipbirds, Spotted Catbirds and Tooth-billed Bowerbirds.

An easy 3 km one-hour walk on a well-maintained level track takes you right around the edge of the lake. About half-way around you get a good view of the lake. Just past here is a fig; a massive, gothic tree with a gnarled root system that has long since consumed its host. About two-thirds around the track is narrow, so take care. There are more lake views from here and an interesting mass of tree roots claw-

Mt Hypipamee National Park is commonly referred to as 'The Crater'. Apart from the distinctive geological formation, featured here also are relatively distinctive forest types including complex notophyll vineforest and simple microphyll vine-fern forest grading into sclerophyll open forest of Brush Box (*Lophostemon confertus*) and Turpentine (*Syncarpia glomulifera*). This gradation is reminiscent of cooler sub-tropical forests of the south-east of the continent.   P. CURTIS

ing their way down the bank towards the water. Around here, also, notice how storm damage can open the forest to an array of pioneer plants which take their opportunity to grow up to the light created by the opening.

Pelicans use the lake, while a variety of birds can be heard or seen. In the lake live the introduced grunters and archer fish which have displaced the rare Lake Eacham Rainbowfish. First identified in 1982 and now driven to extinction in the wild by the new arrivals, it now survives only in captive populations. You can view one of these fish in an aquarium at the Lake Eacham ranger station.

Along the track you may be lucky enough to see the Musky Rat-kangaroo which, by day, is active on the forest floor while at night it sleeps in a nest often made among the roots of trees. Most other mammals are nocturnal, but a good time to see them is early morning or late evening.

Mt Hypipamee National Park

Located 25 km south of Atherton on the Kennedy Highway is a rare example of a volcanic pipe (diatreme) that is surrounded by an unusual type of rainforest. There is a well-maintained picnic area with benches and toilets and a gang of Brush-turkeys which scavenge for scraps from the day trippers. A 400 m track takes you to the diatreme, or 'The Crater' as it is called, and continues 250 m to Dinner Creek before returning to the car park. Allow 40 mins for the circuit.

The high altitude rainforest, growing on red basalt soils, is unique to the area and the forest is rich in species that are similar to those found in sub-tropical rainforests in the south of the state. The wet and cool environment has no doubt contributed to this.

There is also wet sclerophyll forest which you will notice on the other side of the Crater which is dominated by Rose Gum.

Where the track splits to Dinner Falls the soils are derived from granite; note the smaller leaf size of the trees and more uniform size of the tree trunks. Of the 24 species of possum and gliders in Australia seven of them have been found in the forests here. Birds seen here include the Golden Bowerbird, Victoria's Riflebird and various cat-birds.

The Crater, with sheer walls of non-volcanic granite, is the only known example of an explosion pipe on the Tableland. It is about 140m deep, from the top to the bottom. When it was formed thousands of years ago, it did not result in a lava flow, rather it was a vent for the gases which blasted a hole in the rock, sending material flying into the surroundings. The water is covered in a thick layer of duckweed and underneath there is a submerged passage which runs back under the lookout. The pool is home to perch-like fish and crustaceans. Deep silt and tree litter cover the floor which is about 80 m below the surface of the water.

The track continues down to Dinner Falls where a small viewing platform allows for a good view of the white water cascading down the rocks. There is a swimming hole nearby. The track then climbs

A short distance from the car park at Mt Hypipamee National Park, Dinner Creek tumbles over a rock bench to create an attractive cascade. This is a pleasant setting for luncheon 'outings' and one of the traditionally popular spots of the Atherton Tableland.   P. CURTIS

back up the hill returning to the start. For further information contact the QDEH office at Lake Eacham.

Malanda

The Malanda Falls, on the North Johnstone River, drop over the edge of an old lava flow just near the town of Malanda. The basalt here is part of the lava flow which had its origins in the Mt Hypipamee area. This centrally-located town, outside the Wet Tropics Management Area, is a great place to use as a base for a few days on the Tableland.

A unique swimming pool has been created below the falls which has no doubt been the focal point of town life for many years on hot summer days. The camping and caravan park that is adjacent to the Conservation Park is one of the best on the Tableland and a good overnight stopping point. Ask for a spot near the edge of the forest and you will drift off to sleep with the night noises of the animals which make this park their home. Get up early in the morning to take one of the following walks and look out for the wildlife.

Malanda Falls Conservation Park

This short walk (about 20 mins) starts over the road from the Tulip Oak Walk and has named trees, beginning with grand opposing examples of Queensland Maple *(Flindersia brayleana)* and Black Walnut *(Cryptocarya palmerstonii).* It is worth trying to notice the difference in the trees when you are told their names but, be warned, it is really hard to tell the species apart because many of the trunks look alike and the distinguishing signs in the foliage are high above and out of sight. Spare a thought for the botanists whose task to identify rainforest trees often involves shooting down branches to check leaf shapes. The high diversity of plant species is a feature of this forest.

The track follows the edge of the North Johnstone River for a way and just near where you come to the concrete path you will see a big Water Gum being strangled by a fig. Notice the imposing tall tree ferns across the river and look out for a huge Black walnut. The birdlife is prolific in this small forest. Near the end of the trail is a Bumpy Satinash *(Syzygium cormiflorum)* with its tell-tale cauliflory flowering in spring.

Tulip Oak Walk

Over the road from the Conservation Park is a level track beginning from near the picnic area which follows the creek for a short way and where it is possible to see Brush-turkeys and other bird-life, huge birds-nest ferns, a variety of rainforest trees and masses of lawyer cane. This less diverse forest is structurally simpler and has fewer epi-

Noisy Pitta
Pitta versicolor

This brightly coloured bird can be found in rainforests from north of Sydney to the tip of Cape York. Hopping around on the forest floor in search of insects, fruit and, particularly, snails and earthworms, this elusive bird is often hard to spot. Snails are broken open on an 'anvil' rock which is recognisable by the cast aside broken shells.

When they make their distinctive 'walk-to-work' call they are often perched high in the canopy. Noisy Pittas build a large domed nest close to the ground, constructed of twigs, leaves, bark and roots. From three to five spotted eggs are laid and the breeding season runs from October to January.
C. & D. FRITH/FRITHFOTO

phytes, being related to the drier northern forests. As the track swings back around look out for the Tulip Oak tree with a strangler tentacle down one side. Of course, big trees don't last for ever and in the natural process they eventually become decayed and get blown down by strong winds. The biological life of the forest is one of constant renewal as the plants scramble for their place in the light and as natural cycles bring changes to the forest structure. Allow 20 mins for this walk.

The Curtain Fig

From Yungaburra take the Malanda turn-off and travel for 3 km to the roadside car park on the left. As one of the Tableland's top attractions, this site is a very popular destination. One of the largest trees in north Queensland, the Curtain Fig has been formed by a strangler fig *(Ficus destruens)* falling into the crown of a nearby tree which has then become the host tree. From this position the aerial roots have draped down to form the triangular curtain with the myriad of roots welding into one mass and a new crown, nourished by a the massive root sys-

The Curtain Fig is another example of *Ficus virens*. Its distinctive shawl of aerial roots is due to its strangling habit, having germinated from seeds deposited high in the canopy of a host tree which has long since died and decayed.   P. LIK

tem, spread overhead. A boardwalk around the tree stops visitors' feet from trampling the roots and helps cater for the large number of visitors. Scattered around the forest floor are vesicular basalt boulders, which probably saved the site from being cleared in the early days.

DANBULLA FOREST DRIVE

It is possible to stop at a number of places on this 28 km unsealed drive through Danbulla State Forest. The drive can be approached from Tolga on the Kennedy Highway just north of Atherton or from the Gillies Highway just north of the Crater Lakes NP. The road, sealed to the Dam and for the last 4 km before the Gillies Highway, skirts around the Tinaroo Falls Dam which was built in 1958. For those interested in seeing rainforest there are several sites worth visiting. Camping is permitted at several locations with the best being the Kauri Creek camping area which is in a part of the dam where water skiing is not permitted. Be careful driving on the unsealed section of the road after rain. For further information and road conditions contact the QDPI office at Atherton.

Starting from the Atherton end, the drive past the dam lookout will give you views of the dam wall. Seeing the dead trees off to the

The Kauri Creek walk on the Danbulla Forest Drive contains upland rainforest with the stately endemic palm *Oraniopsis appendiculata* a feature.   M. TRENERRY

right is a reminder of the vegetation that the construction of the dam displaced. You will pass Platypus camping area which is set in a Hoop Pine *(Araucaria cunninghamii)* plantation, then Downfall Creek camping area on the edge of the dam, before coming to Kauri Creek camping and picnic area.

Kauri Creek Walk

You can start this moderately strenuous walk from three points. There is a small parking area just a couple of hundred metres on the left past the turn-off to the Kauri Creek camping area. There is also a day-use area with all facilities just 100 m further on past this parking area which would enable you to walk back to the start of the track. Third, if you wish to start from the camping area, a track leads off from near the the toilet block, through a plantation for 400 m then crosses the main road to the beginning of the rainforest walk.

The track, a 5 km circuit, follows Kauri Creek for a way then leads up a steep ridge and continues down, with a couple of creek crossings, to meet an old logging road which you walk back down. A trail then leads back into the forest to meet your starting point. Allow 2 hours for this top class walk. An alternative to the circuit, which still includes the best features, is to return back the way you came after the

---

Crater lakes or 'maars' are a legacy of the volcanic activity which formed much of the present landscape and influenced the vegetation of the Atherton Tableland. Lake Euramoo, shown here, has also been a very useful pollen trap from which sediments have been drawn to reconstruct the vegetation history of the area.   R. RITCHIE

ascent of the ridge. This way you will avoid having to take your shoes off to ford a couple of creek crossings that have no bridges. On the other hand you will miss seeing the full diversity of this rainforest remnant. After rain this track can be greasy, so take care. This is a diverse rainforest with a range of plants and animals including Red Cedar, White Cockatoos and Wompoo Pigeons. An endemic palm *Oraniopsis apendiculata* is also found here.

The track climbs for a short distance after leaving Kauri Creek. Here Brown Salwood Wattle *(Acacia aulacocarpa)* is regenerating after the area was previously cleared for grazing. Hoop Pines have been planted at the start of the walk along the side of a hill which leads down to cross a creek and where the vegetation changes to rainforest. The mass of lawyer vine here indicates past disturbance to the forest. Not far in is a short side track to a Red Cedar that was spared earlier logging because of its forked branches. Soon after is a clearing where an old tree has fallen, pulling vines off surrounding trees. Notice how the small pioneer seedling plants have sprung up to fill the gap.

After about 15 mins of walking you see the sandy bottomed Kauri Creek again. Look for the big fig in a swampy part of the track plus the distinctive endemic palms. When you come to a junction in the track take the left fork to begin the circuit. After about 40 mins from the start you will reach the top of the steep ridge. As mentioned, an option here is to return the same way.

Continuing on the very steep path of an old snig trail leads down the hill. The bird life is prolific. At the bottom you have to cross Kauri Creek where you will get your feet wet. Look out for more of the endemic palms. You now come to an old logging road which winds back in a southerly direction and gives you a chance to look down into the forest.

After 20 mins on this road, an unsignposted track leads off to the right and back into the regrowth forest where the exotic Lantana *(Lantana camera)* and a few native species are competing to reclaim cleared land. There is another small creek crossing and you are back into rainforest. The final crossing of Kauri Creek will bring you to the track junction and the 1 km walk back to your starting point.

For further information contact the QDPI office at Atherton.

Lake Euramoo

This crater lake, or more properly 'swamp', is easily viewed from an observation platform. As well, there is a 400 m loop track with labelled trees passing through rainforest on the lake's edge. The interior rim of the lake was terraced during World War II to create an amphitheatre

The sylvan setting of Mobo Creek, with its puzzling volcanic origins, is easily reached from the Danbulla Forest Drive.   R. RITCHIE

where spectators watched aquatic carnivals put on by the Army.

The interpretative sign indicates that the lake is contained in a double explosion volcanic crater. One of the youngest geological features on the Atherton Tableland, the lake is only 10,000 years old. Carbon dating of sediment samples from different depths has given scientists an idea of the changes in vegetation by counting the different types of pollen in the sediments. From specific time periods they are able to build an idea of the type of vegetation existing: 60,000–30,000 years ago the Tableland was dominated by rainforest similar to today's Hoop Pine forest in South-east Queensland; 30,000–9000 years ago the Tableland was dominated by drier open forests; while 9000–present the vegetation became more tropical.

Mobo Creek Crater

This 600 m circular track leading to Mobo Crater begins from the car park and is a very easy, short walk. This recently upgraded trail winds down to Mobo Creek. Along the way some of the trees are marked including the Brown Tulip Oak *(Aryrodendron polyandrum)* and White Beech *(Gmelina dalrympleana)*.

The basaltic rocky creek flows into a small crater which has posed a problem for geologists because the rocks appear to be 'flowing' into, rather than out of, the crater. Also the steep walls of the crater consist of non-volcanic rocks rather than the expected basalt. One explanation is that the crater represents the remnant of an underground basalt formation, and over time the waters of Mobo Creek have eroded the non-volcanic rock above this formation exposing the basalt, hence the basalt rock now forms the creek base. A sign on location explains the phenomena in more detail.

On the way back look for the cauliflory on the Bumpy Satinash in spring and a huge Brush-turkey mound. Allow at least 20 mins for the walk.

The Cathedral Fig

This popular spot is the last attraction on the Danbulla Forest Drive from the Atherton end or the first (about 5 km in) if you are approaching from the Gillies Highway.

A 100 m walk leads to this 500 year-old Green Fig *(Ficus virens)* with many of the species named along the way. As high as a twelve-storey building, with a crown extending over .2 ha and with a girth of 43 m, this tree fulfils all the criteria for that

A superb specimen of *Ficus virens*, The Cathedral Fig stands in complex notophyll vine forest growing on krasnozem soils derived from basalts.

This is a forest type which once was extensive on the Atherton Tableland but is now practically all cleared. This, along with a tiny reserve near Tolga and some fragments in State Forest near Wongabel is essentially all that remains.

A major attraction on the Danbulla Forest Drive, this tree is home to a variety of rainforest fauna.   R. RITCHIE

must-see spectacle. Roots which have the look of cathedral flying buttresses have no doubt given this tree its name although it has been suggested that the cross-like shape of the branches was the inspiration.

With the host tree long rotted out, the tree has a cavernous interior and wildlife relies on the tree as a refuge. Victoria's Riflebird, Big-spotted Catbird, Boyd's Forest Dragon and even pythons have been observed in the daytime while at night Lumholtz's Tree-kangaroo, small Sugar Gliders and Green Ring-tailed possums have all been spotted. On the ground, Long-nosed Bandicoots, Red-legged Pademelons and Musky Rat-kangaroos can be seen at dawn or dusk.

The verdant hills of the Atherton Tableland stretch into the distance from Millaa Millaa Lookout. This is an extensive agricultural area which was developed at the turn of the last century due to the existence of rich soils derived from basalt. Evidence of the source of these volcanic parent materials occurs as eruption mounds and craters scattered across the Tableland.   P. LIK

Tully Gorge National Park

A narrow, winding strip of bitumen takes you 24 km into a large tract of rainforest centred on the Upper Tully Gorge, southeast of the old timber town of Ravenshoe. The good access to this otherwise remote corner of the Wet Tropics is due to the construction of the Koombooloomba Dam, Weir and, far below, the Kareeya Hydro-Electric Power Station. The once wild spectacle of Tully Falls has, like Barron Falls, been tempered due to the water storage and diversion through the mountain to the turbines below.

Due, in main, to the absence of the central feature of the water-fall, a once extensive walking track system to vantage points over the gorge and falls has deteriorated to almost non-existence. Facilities are, however, maintained at the carpark at Tully Falls National Park where a 1 km walking trail takes you to the river above the falls. Despite the usual lack of water the views from the carpark lookout and the top of the falls are breathtaking. The short rockhop to the head of the falls must be undertaken with care and only when the rocks are dry.

A 350 m walk upstream brings you to the weir where the out-flow from the dam is ponded before commencing its drop to the hydro station at Kareeya. Crossing the weir, follow the road east by foot or car for about 2 km for another magnificent panorama. Here, at the end of the road, a cable car for the use of QEC staff only descends steeply to Kareeya Station below.

Back at the Ravenshoe–Koombooloomba Dam Road it is about 19 km further along the road from the Tully Falls turn-off to Koombooloomba Dam. Picnic and camping facilities are provided and its extensive backwaters are excellent for exploring by canoe, particularly when the water level is high at the end of the Wet Season.

OTHER PLACES TO VISIT

Wongabel State Forest

Only 8 km south of Atherton, on the eastern side of the Kennedy Highway, is the Wongabel Botanical Walk. With the aid of a pamphlet available at the start of the walk or from the QDPI office in Atherton, you will be able to identify 191 trees along the 2.6 km walk.

Bromfield Swamp

Five minutes drive down the road from Lake Eacham is another volcanic crater which has been worn down by erosion and formed into a lake. It is similar to Lakes Eacham and Barrine except that the rainforest has been cleared from around it and a swamp has developed from sediments formed by erosion of the crater. There is no walk here because the site is private property; just a place to pull off the road and look down over this unique wetland habitat. It is possible for scientists to investigate the climate and vegetation history of the swamp and its surroundings by looking at sediment layers and using carbon dating techniques.

An interpretative sign on location puts the lake in geological context: 10,500 years ago when the climate was drier, the vegetation around this swamp was eucalypt forest with she oaks as an understorey. This has been confirmed by taking samples from up to 8 m in depth. 8500 years ago cool, wet forests began to form around the swamp. Common species were Pimply Ash *(Balanops australiana)*, Quandong, Coachwoods *(Ceratopetalum spp.)* and Climbing Pandanus *(Freyeinetia* spp.). Today, many of these species can be found at higher altitudes in north Queensland. About 2500 years ago the vegetation reverted to a warmer and drier rainforest type, which can now be seen at Wongaville State Forest and Yungaburra State Forest.

Common waterbirds found here include brolgas, magpie geese, and wild ducks. Many birds make an annual journey from the Gulf of

Carpentaria to feed on the paddocks of the Tableland. In winter, at sunset, hundreds of brolgas and cranes fly in to roost, giving the lucky spectator a magnificent sight.

Millstream Falls National Park

Located just west of Ravenshoe, this popular day-trip destination is also claimed as Australia's widest waterfall and it is indeed an impressive sight after rain as the water tumbles over the edge of the solidified basalt lava flow.

Notice the dry open woodland vegetation of the park which is the result of its location in a rain shadow of the ranges. This allows for a regime of fire which basically ensures no rainforest plant life. The distinctive stringybarks, ironbarks and bloodwoods predominate.

Good park facilities are provided and walking tracks lead down to several popular swimming spots. For further details contact the QDEH office at Lake Eacham.

Millaa Millaa Falls Waterfall Circuit

East of the southern Tableland from the town of Millaa Millaa, Scenic Route 9 (also known as Theresa Creek Road) takes you on a winding journey through lush pastures right past three easily accessible water-falls in natural rainforest surrounds.

Just out of the town a signpost on the highway directs you to Millaa Millaa Falls along the Waterfall Circuit. Just 2 km from the highway you come to Millaa Millaa Falls, one of the most pho-tographed falls of all. From the carpark a grassy spit protrudes into the green amphitheatre where the delicate veil of water is the centre of attention. A short 100 m circuit track winds through the tall rainforest remnant near the picnic facilities.

Continuing along the Scenic Route, Zillie Falls comes up after about 8 km. There is a covered picnic site at the carpark on one side of the road and a track commences on the other side to take you to a number of lookouts over the falls. The track descends to near the bottom of the falls where the spray from the waterfall ensures the surrounding rock faces are always dripping with life. Consequently, this area is always slippery and hazardous. The best idea is to progress only to where you feel safe.

Back on the road again you continue for another 2.5 km, watching out for signs directing you to Elinjaa Falls. A 100 m walk com-

---

Exposed to a constant spray of water droplets, the vegetation in the splash zone of waterfalls such as Zillie, shown here, is composed of hydrophytes or water-loving plants which include ferns and mosses.   P. LIK

mences from a pleasantly landscaped picnic area and again descends to the bottom of the falls. This time, in a perfectly safe environment, you can stand at a bracing viewpoint in front of the waterfall for another photo opportunity. A further 3.4 km along the road takes you back to the highway.

All the falls have a good year-round flow and are individually attractive. Swimming is good at Millaa Millaa Falls, passable at Elinjaa and not recommended at Zillie. Overall, this trip is an ideal opportunity to take in some good scenery in a short time and distance, with little or no difficulty for the very young or those infirmed.

These collections of fruits from two geographic locations represent just some of the hundreds of different native fruits found in the Wet Tropics. They were gathered in the month of January. The brightly coloured fruits have evolved primarily to attract animals, particularly birds and fruit bats, which disperse the seeds and thereby ensure the survival of the plant. Birds are able to see colours, but with few exceptions, are unable to smell. Fruit bats, on the other hand, are colour blind but have an acute sense of smell. Cassowaries are responsible for dispersing more than 100 species of trees and vines.

Aborigines supplemented their diets with edible fruits, while poisonous seeds were pounded and leached in running water before being prepared into food. The early settlers also soon learned to complement their often bland diets with rainforest fruits. However, the potential commercial value of fruits was largely ignored until recent times when the interest in indigenous cooking ingredients developed. This is providing an incentive for horticulturalists to propagate and cultivate selected plants.

Some of the fruits and their uses include: from the uplands, Russell River Limes (jams) and Atherton Oaks (sauces). From the lowland: Crab Apples (jams), White Apples (edible raw), Burdekin Plums (jams) and Davidson's Plum (sauces and jams).

Remember, never attempt to eat fruits unless you have properly identified them. Fruit from the Finger Cherry (Rhodomyrtus macrocarpa), for example, has been known to cause blindness. When in doubt it is best to leave them well alone.

M. TRENERRY

Fruits of the Forest

UPLANDS

LOWLANDS

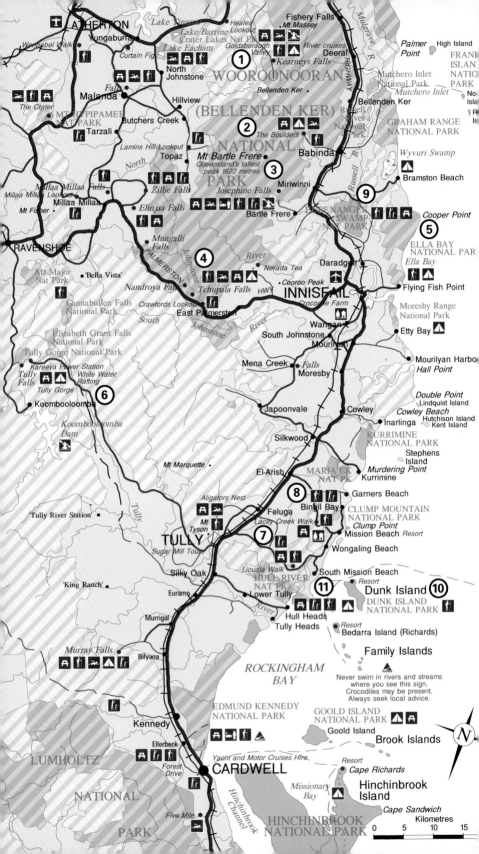

INNISFAIL

TULLY

OTHER PLACES

INNISFAIL/TULLY

To the Giramay people of the Tully district, living in the wettest region of Australia, the rainforest was a storehouse of plant foods and the rivers a source of fish. The seeds from Black Pines and Zamias were pounded into flour while toxic seeds were prepared and leached in bags in flowing streams to make them palatable. The women also used lawyer-cane dilly bags to catch the small fish which made their way upstream during flood times.

Like elsewhere, food gathering was the major chore. Ingenious methods devised by hunters included waiting in trees with a long stick to knock flying foxes to the ground. On the coast, the low-flying Torres Strait Pigeons were similarly dispatched as they flew low over the water on their way homewards to the islands. To the south, the Mamu people of the Johnstone River district paddled their outrigger canoes offshore in search of turtle and dugong.

This wet region also posed problems for the newcomers. In 1882, the seasoned rainforest traveller, Christie Palmerston, was engaged by the local Divisional Board to explore the rugged country between Innisfail (then called Geraldton) and Herberton for a possible railway route. The journey, through 80 km of dense tropical rainforest, took 12 days. An extract from his diary gives some idea of the conditions encountered on the trek:

> Still raining. Started again through this dreary stretch of blackness in a north-westerly direction over a basalt tableland covered with dense jungle. In about three miles ran foul of another precipice, could hear the roar of impetuous waters hundreds of feet below me. Rain, rain, everywhere I try to look there is a black patch between me and the object I wish to look at. Turned south-ward again and had level travelling all afternoon, gradually worked my way north-west again and in two miles struck a large river, the Beatrice, the bed of it being full of large boulders, current broad and very strong. Camped here, raining so fast, and so piercingly cold that my companions limbs are thoroughly numb.

Late last century the journalist and explorer, Archibald Meston, foresaw a great recreation potential for the lower ravines of Mt Bellenden Ker. He thought the Morehead Cataracts would be a 'future paradise of the artist and the lovers of the beautiful; the scenery-hunting tourists of years to come' when they became 'familiar to the outside world of amateur explorers'. But he despaired about the consequences of this, because visitors had a tendency to leave their 'sardine tins… sandwich wrappers, and infernal rum bottles' at the site.

Meston led a plant and animal collecting expedition to the Bellenden Ker Ranges in 1889. In many ways an enlightened person for his times, Meston made special efforts to find out the Aboriginal names for the natural features. He hoped they would be adopted not only for unnamed places, but to supersede many of the 'utterly meaningless names already conferred by surveyors and local residents'.

Meston's wish has come true with Bellenden Ker National Park having just had its name changed to Wooroonooran.

Hundreds of specimens were collected on this trip. Many new plants were found, including a native mangosteen *(Garcinia mestonii)* which Meston thought had a 'very pleasant' taste, and would be a 'valuable addition to the fruits of the world'. The seeds of this and other fruiting plants were brought back in the hope they could be propagated for future commercial use.

The town of Innisfail took its name from that of the first plantation in the district. A succession of migrant farmers from Ireland, China and, in later years, Italy, cleared the rainforests and farmed the land for bananas and sugar cane. Positioned at the junction of the north and south arms of the Johnstone River it is today a service town for a rich agricultural district. While it is understandable that early settlers had few options but to clear land, it is incredible that just 20 years ago 16,480 ha of lowland rainforest was cleared in the Tully River Valley by US interests for the King Ranch cattle venture.

On the coast, the town of Mission Beach has a history that is

---

The Ulysses Butterfly, with its metallic blue and jet black wings is a common sight in the Wet Tropics and especially Dunk Island. RAINFOREST HABITAT

linked to the efforts of the Cutten family to found a tropical plantation at Bingal Bay in the 1880s. Using Aboriginal labour they cleared the rainforests that grew here down to the shore and planted tea, coffee, mangoes and coconut palms and a host of other crops. In 1918 disaster struck in the form of a severe cyclone and its accompanying tidal wave which all but wiped out the settlement. Interestingly, it was the remnant tea bushes which provided the cuttings for the Nerada tea plantation at the foothills of the Bellenden Ker Range. This cyclone also flattened the Aboriginal mission which had been established just four years earlier near the mouth of the Hull River.

Today, Mission Beach is a popular little town with rainforest growing down to the sea and with holiday homes dotting the hillsides. A good variety of accommodation is on offer including popular hostels. An information centre run by the Community for Coastal and Cassowary Conservation is well worth visiting.

Goldsborough Valley State Forest

This state forest is part of the Mulgrave River valley below the Bellenden Ker Range. From Gordonvale take the Gillies Highway and look for the Goldsborough Valley turn-off 6 km out. Travel 15 km, over half on a bumpy gravel road, to a large, well maintained day and camping area with all amenities.

The scenic drive passes many swimming holes accessible to visitors. This popular recreation area also provides open, grassy areas for sport and many access points to the wide (but not very deep) Mulgrave River. This river is unsurpassed as a venue for canoeists who prefer relaxation and scenery to excitement. An idyllic half-day can be spent paddling/drifting down to the highway and beyond (some short portages are necessary). From the campground you can take a short walk to Kearneys Falls or the one-day walk on the Goldfield Trail to The Boulders near Babinda. For further information contact the QDPI office in Atherton or the QDEH office in Innisfail.

Kearneys Falls Walk

Kearney's Falls tumbles down the slopes of Mt Bellenden Ker and passes right through the park. A 870 m easy walking track through lowland tropical rainforest leads to the Falls. Try this walk late in the afternoon when the low light dapples the tree trunks and illuminates the

The Goldsborough Valley, situated just over 20 km south of Cairns, has a rich and varied history which has included gold mining and logging activities. Signs of this disturbance include not only relics of machinery and other equipment but in the prevalence of plants such as the ever-present Lawyer Cane or Wait-a-while (*Calamus* spp.) which thrives once the canopy is opened.   PETER LIK

Major changes in vegetation are reflected in the differing topography at Mt Bellenden Ker, from the 1622 m peak to the valley of the Mulgrave River as it flows to the sea. On the summit there are windswept low moss fern thickets and heathlands, while tall complex meso-phyll vineforest towers over the river's lower reaches.   P. CURTIS

westerly facing falls. Signs interpreting Aboriginal life give you an idea of how the Malanbarra clan, many of whom still live in the district, used the forest. Look out for the Scrub Fowl mound at the beginning of the walk. Many large figs are evident from the rocky pathway through the forest including a massively buttressed specimen, after about 15 mins, just at the top of a stairway.

Kearneys Falls, known to the local people as 'Wajil', forms the basis for a legend which infuses the landscape with a mythical significance. In the Wet Season the Malanbarra people camped at the top of the falls, where food such a Brush-turkey eggs and seeds were available. A steep track leads up to a vantage point over the falls, but be careful here.

There are some deep pools at the base of the falls, however, do observe the warning signs and take due care on the slippery rock faces. Allow at least 1 hour for the walk and put aside some time to observe the variety of plant life in this special place.

Goldfield Trail,
Goldsborough Valley

An opportunity to experience a transect of the rainforest wilderness, that is the Bellenden Ker section of Wooroonooran National Park, may be taken by walking along the Goldfield Trail between the Goldsborough Valley State Forest Park and Babinda Boulders Wildland Park. This trail was blazed in the 1930s by gold prospectors eager to reach the north-western slopes of Mt Bartle Frere where there was the promise of a field opening up. Reopened in 1986, the track traverses the relatively low saddle between the heights of Mts Bellenden Ker and Bartle Frere.

Highlights of the walk include the chance to see a wide variety of vegetation types, some possible animal sightings and superlative views over the surrounding countryside.

The walk along the Goldfield Trail can be accomplished from either end with the following considerations. You can either arrange to be collected at the end of the walk and returned to your car or make it a return overnight trip. There is an excellent campsite on the Mulgrave River on the western side at the 'causeway', which is 8 km from the Forest Park and 11 km from The Boulders, or further downstream at the main campground at the car park.

Alternatively, you can walk west to east and camp at the council campground near the Boulders. A third option would be to walk in and back to the causeway from either end, a relatively easy walk of 16

Southern Cassowary
Casuarius casuarius

This large, flightless bird with its distinctive red and blue neck belongs to the most primitive group of living birds, the Ratites. The other member of this group in Australia is the Emu. Living off about 70 species of fallen fruits of the rainforest, they are found from Paluma to Cape York. Two other species live in New Guinea. Mostly shy, they are only likely to become aggressive if they are protecting eggs or young. In the Wet Tropics there are several locations where relatively tame birds may be observed in the wild.

The coarse blue-black plumage is well anchored to resist the wear and tear of the forest while the adult's bony 'helmet' acts as a form of protection to a bird which, without wings, often travels at speed through the prickly rainforest. Spike-like nails on their huge toes have developed as a form of defence and they are able to inflict great harm if they so choose. Cassowaries remain solitary for most of the year.

Female birds are the dominant sex, being taller, heavier and more brightly coloured and, apart from the breeding season, they appear to scorn males. After the female lays her three to five

blue-green eggs, the male takes charge of the nest tending and rearing of the young. The striped downy, brown feathers of the chicks make them hard to spot on the forest floor and it takes them three years to attain their full adult plumage. M. PROCIV

Waterfalls are often places which support a variety of special plant life because of the particular microclimate which is created by the constant dampness provided by the fine mist of spray. A year-round spectacle, Nandroya Falls drop 40 m into a large pool before spilling over in a cascade that feeds Douglas Creek.   R. RITCHIE

km return from the Forest Park or a more arduous walk of 22 km return from The Boulders. The Goldfield Trail brochure put out by QDEH provides a useful map.

If, like most people, you are walking one way it would be wise to avoid undertaking the journey immediately after periods of heavy or extended rain as the causeway on the Mulgrave River may be impassable. Devise a contingency plan so you don't have your pick-up person worrying unnecessarily. Unfortunately for some, despite the road between the Goldsborough campground and the causeway being recently improved, it has nonetheless been closed to all traffic meaning an extra two hours walking. Because of this, it is recommended a one-way walk be undertaken from the Goldsborough side.

Although not unduly steep (the track rises to about 340 m at the saddle) it is 19 km long and takes the best part of a day if you take your time. If walking from the Boulders and you are feeling just a little fatigued, when you get to the causeway, the remaining 8 km walk along the well-constructed forestry road (usually teeming with motor bikes on weekends) is easier going.

Overall, this is one of the best of the long-distance walks in north Queensland and the relatively easy grades traverse some magnificent forests and cross a number of refreshing streams. Of particular interest is the presence of some of the King Fern *(Angiopteris evecta)*. With fronds up to seven metres long they are reputed to be the longest of any fern in the world.

Along the waterways the trees of the lowland rainforests are festooned with epiphytes. Apart from the obvious screams of the Sulphur-crested Cockatoos and the scratchings of the Brush-turkey, it is worth looking out for some of the smaller birds, such as the scrub-wrens and thornbills which inhabit the forests.

One word of warning – don't underestimate your need for water when walking in this environment. As most of the walk is at low altitude temperatures and humidity can be very high at all times of the year. Despite a number of creek crossings it is essential to carry water and drink some at every opportunity.

The Boulders Wildland Park

Just 7 km west of the Bruce Highway at the small town of Babinda, this small council reserve is a good place to experience the complex rainforests adjacent to Wooroonooran National Park. With an annual rainfall of over 6000 mm the water that cascades down the mountains has strewn huge boulders along the creek. Rich in plant and bird-life, this reserve has two short walks and is the start (or finish) of the

The contorted water-worn roots of this Water Gum (*Tristaniopsis exiliflora*) at The Boulders add to the power, mystery and intricacy of a place which is infused with Aboriginal legend.   P. CURTIS

Goldfield Trail. A well-developed picnic area has natural swimming holes, barbecues and toilets. Just outside the reserve there is a council camping ground.

Devils Pool Walk and Boulders Gorge Lookout
This is one of the most popular scenic/swimming spots in the north. A number of deep, refreshing pools commence only metres from the car park. There are many signs about the dangers of swimming here but the best warning is a poignant memorial stone at the beginning of the walk: 'Pray for the soul of Pat McGann/He came for a visit 22-6-79/and stayed forever'.

An Aboriginal legend has it that a young woman named Oolana threw herself into the stream on being separated from her lover. To this day she calls young men to their doom and, over the years, many have obliged her.

A pleasant walking track, which follows the sandy-bottomed arm of Babinda Creek for 470 m, brings you to a view over Devils Pool and a further 130 m walk leads to Boulders Gorge Lookout where water rushes away down a small gorge.

Wonga Track
This short lowland rainforest circuit walk, with named trees, is dedicated to the Wonga family, long-term Aboriginal residents of the district. Across the suspension bridge over Babinda Creek, is the start of the 850 m track which follows the creek. The track can be wet because this is a flood-prone area, so be prepared for heavy going. A few species have numbers which can be identified by referring to the brochure which should be available at the park. About half-way there is a cleared spot with a view across another creek and from here the path circles back along its bank to the suspension bridge.

Wooroonooran National Park
One of Queensland's largest rainforest national parks, it includes the state's two highest mountains, Mt Bartle Frere (1622 m) and Mt Bellenden Ker (1582 m). This park of 79,500 ha includes the Bellenden Ker and Palmerston Sections, creating a massive protected rainforested wilderness of peaks, gorges and plateaux of great spectacle and scientific importance.

Because of the differing elevations there are many types of vegetation within the park; from dense lowland forests to cyclone-damaged

---

Lianes or ropey woody vines give rainforests a character so unlike Australia's open forests. They use the trees for support in their climb towards the light in the upper canopy so they may get on with the business of growth and reproduction. P. LIK

This strangler fig has commenced its life as a germling on a branch of a host tree high in the canopy of the rich forests of the Palmerston section of Wooroonooran National Park. Here there is light to drive photosynthesis and to produce roots which it sends down to the ground. This fig eventually enveloped its host, which has long died and decomposed. R. RITCHIE

slopes, on to wind-swept, low heath on the peaks above 1500m. The top of Bartle Frere is a complex of peaks and hanging valleys; of bald heathy slopes and huge, black lichen-covered boulders.

Mt Bartle Frere was first climbed in 1886 by the venturesome Christie Palmerston. He continued the time-honoured tradition of carving his name in a tree at the summit.

Interestingly, the local Aborigines, while being known to climb the slopes, would never attempt the climb to the summit of these mountains. The reverence they held for them was tinged with a fear that the great spirit Murgalainya would one day return to its nesting place.

Today, as the pressures of dozens of tramping climbers make their ascent on Bartle Frere, naturalists are hoping that a modern-day taboo can dissuade many from the journey. There is a real threat that introduced pathogens, brought in on the boots of walkers, will upset the delicate ecological balance on the upper parts of the ranges.

Bellenden Ker Section

Josephine Falls Track

Look for the turn-off 66 km south of Cairns and travel another 8 km to the picnic area with covered sheds and toilets. Camping is not permitted here. An 800 m, easy walk to Josephine Falls leads through lowland rainforest. Three different viewing spots give good views of the falls which are quite impressive year-round.

Broken Nose

Broken Nose is a major peak on the southern flanks of Mt Bartle Frere. From the picnic area it is possible to walk to this place which, for most people, will be a sufficient introduction to the park. A comparatively easy walk, but through rough terrain, of just over an hour leads for 3 km to the Majuba Creek campsite at the second crossing of this creek. Just before the campsite is a turn-off to the left where the track, which is steep in places, leads off for a strenuous one-and-half hour walk up to the 'snout' of the aptly-named Broken Nose.

From its 962 m summit the walker is presented with impressive views of the pristine Russell River valley and Mt Bartle Frere. It is worth trying to distinguish the different types of vegetation that this elevated view of the forest offers. Allow about 7 hours for the 10 km return journey to Broken Nose.

Mt Bartle Frere
The summit is an arduous 15 km return journey, taking a full day, which can be dangerous in the bad weather that can close in on the mountain at any time of the year. It should only be attempted by fit and experienced walkers. Access is possible from the picnic area via Majuba Creek campsite and the walk to the summit and return takes about 12 hours.

Palmerston Section

Located astride the Palmerston Highway, which leads to the Atherton Tableland, 33 km west of Innisfail and 30 km south-east of Millaa Millaa, are some of the best walks in the Wet Tropics with a variety of rainforest scenery.

Crawfords Lookout to Tchupalla Falls Walk
The small clearing at Crawfords Lookout allows a striking view over the Johnstone Valley. From here it is possible to walk to Tchupalla Falls (4.2 km) and on to Henrietta Creek picnic area (an extra 2.4 km). From the lookout the track winds down into North Johnstone Gorge before following the contour line of the hills, past Cedar Falls, and parallel to Douglas and Henrietta Creeks. This reasonably strenuous walk, which involves some steep sections, is best attempted after making arrangements to be picked up at either Tchupalla Falls or Henrietta Creek picnic area.

Tchupalla Falls and Wallicher Falls Walks
An easier way to get to Tchupalla Falls and the neighbouring Wallicher Falls is to proceed 2 km further west from Crawfords Lookout to a small parking area on the north side of the Palmerston Highway. This spot used to be called the K-Tree. From here begins two short walks to these picturesque waterfalls. If you are short of time then the Tchupalla Falls walk is the more scenic.

To visit Wallicher Falls take the left fork just after the beginning and a level 800 m trail leads to a viewing spot above the falls. A further 200 m leads to a ford above the falls. The track from here leads to the Henrietta Creek camping area. However, to visit Tchupalla Falls retrace your steps to the junction.

From here the other fork leads to a viewing spot overlooking Tchupalla Falls. Along the way there are numbered trees that are identifiable with the aid of a brochure available at the start of the walk. Tree number four, a huge Milky Pine *(Alstonia scholaris)*, is one of a number of forest giants which serve as a reminder of what these forests were like before the timber-getters arrived.

At the falls viewing spot, the prominent, lichen-draped tree is sustained by the fine mist which comes from the falls. Past the lookout is a series of steep steps which lead you to views of the basalt gorge and further falls where Henrietta Creek joins Douglas Creek which tumbles down on its way to join the North Johnstone River. The trail leads on for 4.2 km to Crawfords Lookout, but for the purposes of this walk you may retrace your steps back to the parking area.

Nandroya Falls Walk
This 4.8 km return or 7.2 km circuit walk is one of the best medium distance walks in the Wet Tropics. The camping/day use area at Henrietta Creek is the starting point, but if you wish to avoid getting

The easily accessible Tchupalla Falls on Henrietta Creek is one of the most idyllic and picturesque of the many waterfalls in the Wet Tropics. R. RITCHIE

wet feet crossing the creek, walk west along the highway about 300 m and off into the forest where you can easily pick up the trail. The track can be boggy after rain so proceed with care.

About 500 m along you come to a fork in the track, take the left branch and after 1 km of easy walking you come to Silver Falls with its impressive semi-circular rock wall. Musky Rat-kangaroos can often be heard, and sometimes seen, as they scratch around for food. Keep an eye (and ear) out for King Parrots, a variety of pigeons, honeyeaters and, especially, Victoria's Riflebird, which is often spotted on this walk.

Following the track you look down into a deep ravine off to your right. Within 500 m you come to Douglas Creek and the impressive Nandroya Falls with its 40 m main drop and large pool of water which spills out, tumbling over a large rock face to smaller falls.

From here you have two options for the return. The first is to retrace your steps and walk the 2.4 km back, while the other is a 3.6 km diversion which follows Douglas Creek before swinging back over a hill to rejoin the original track. This track requires more care as it is not as well formed to begin with. However, don't be put off if you or your party are feeling up to the slightly longer return journey. It is well worth the effort.

Along this walk the Douglas Creek is seen off to the left as it cascades down a variety of waterfalls. After about 10 mins you come to the riverbank which could be a good place for a snack break. Not far past here the river suddenly falls away to almost fade from view.

The track moves away from the river and you come to a spot where you can see into the canopy of the rainforest on the other side of the bank. Just on your right, look out for a cascade of solidified lava in the form of a patterned basalt outcrop. Just past here is a small grotto, complete with its own waterfall. After a climb out of it, the track levels out for easy walking.

After one hour's walk you should be back to the fork where you retrace your steps back to the campground. Allow at least two-and-a-half hours for the full walk.

Ella Bay National Park

East of Innisfail, a short drive along the north bank of the Johnstone River passes through the township of The Coconuts and then, after only about 5 km, you come to Flying Fish Point at the river mouth. Following the signs north, the road skirts a rainforest headland (similar to parts of the Cape Tribulation Road) and provides tantalising glimpses through the trees of sandy beaches stretching north into the distance, broken by small rocky intrusions backed by rainforest-clad hills. However, like Cape Tribulation, much of the land is private property and the park boundary is irregular. The road descends to a picturesque beach at the southern end of Ella Bay where the Johnstone Shire Council allows small-scale camping. No facilities are provided and an inspector collects fees in the evenings.

Further vehicular progress north is prevented by a locked gate where the private property begins. However, at this point, put on some sandshoes, sunscreen and a hat and commence one of north Queensland's great tropical beach walks. The beach is about 9 km long and it doesn't take long before other footprints start to disappear and you can appreciate how easy it is in the north to find yourself alone in an expansive natural area.

The national park boundary recommences shortly after a creek outflow about 30 mins from the carpark. Another 45 mins brings you to a small headland and a further 40 mins to where Cooper Creek out-flows below Cooper Point. It is not practical to walk beyond this point. A vast paperbark wetland lies behind the beach and within this broad ecosystem are many other forest types that vary with small changes in elevation. If setting out on an Ella Bay journey take ample water and sun protection with you. Possible environmental hazards are marine stingers and Estuarine Crocodiles. Also, remember not to leave any valuables in your vehicle. This walk is about 4 hours return.

Tully State Forest
About 40 mins scenic drive north-west of Tully, the upper reaches of the Tully River have been developed for rafting. At the end of the road is the hydro-electricity station and a couple of kilometres before it is an excellent camping area with all facilities. From here there is raft access and walkways to the river. About the only activity for non-rafters is to take a walk along the riverbank. Remember Tully River levels change quickly and at any time without notice. Back along the road to Tully is a lookout which provides good views over a bend in the river.

Tam O'Shanter State Forest
Lacey Creek Forest Walk
On the El Arish–Mission Beach Road, about 5 km from the Bruce Highway, is the Lacey Creek forest walk. There are good picnic facilities here and a swimming hole.

The 1 km easy circuit walk is through lowland rainforest and has information boards to explain the importance of the forest to Cassowaries which may be seen here in the early morning or evening.

Wild rivers are a feature of the eastern section of the Wet Tropics where streams plunge down the steep ranges on their short path to the sea. The Tully River Valley is a place renown for its adventure activities which include long hikes through rugged country and white-water rafting.   R. RITCHIE

With almost all the original lowland rainforest cleared for agriculture, this and the adjacent forests are important Cassowary habitats. Look out for the Alexandra Palms *(Archontophoenix alexandra)* growing by the creek. A viewing platform over the creek offers a chance to spot some aquatic life, where you may see tortoises, giant prawns and several species of fish.

A 7 km track, beginning over the road opposite the entrance, links Lacey Creek with Licuala SF Park in the south. Along the way there is a track which leads to Luff Hill Lookout with views over Mission Beach and out to the islands.

Licuala State Forest Park

Although it is possible to walk south from Lacey Creek, the main entrance to this park is from the Mission Beach–Tully Road where a turn-off to the right about 6 km from Mission Beach, leads you in to the park entrance. As one of the best remaining examples of lowland Fan Palm *(Licuala ramsayi)* forest and as the best place to have a chance of seeing Cassowaries, this park is highly recommended.

There is a short walk on the right just a few hundred metres in from the main road. Look out for it as it is easy to miss. The 536 m Licuala Fan Palm Boardwalk includes information boards on this unique form of vegetation. Only small patches of this rainforest between here and the Daintree (which thrives on poorly drained alluvial soil) have survived clearing and about half of the existing forest is in the area between Stoney Creek, North Hull River and O'Donnell Creek. Few plants are able to withstand such waterlogged conditions. The canopy is almost entirely fan palms reaching 10-15 m.

Just further on is a car park where a level 7 km walk leads to the Licuala Creek Forest Walk. Following an old logging track it is possible to walk all or part of this track, which crosses several creeks and passes through a variety of forest types. As well, this special forest is home to many bird species which may come into view along the track. Near the first bridge over the Hull River there is a swimming hole. Further on there are good views from Luff Hill Lookout.

The Licuala Creek Walk in Tam O'Shanter State Forest allows visitors to experience an almost monospecific stand of fan palms (*Licuala ramsayi*). Such forests reach their best development within the very wet coastal lowlands and are nowhere better developed than they appear here. The plump fruits of these palms are favoured Cassowary food during the months of November and December.

The various forest walks in this state forest pass through a variety of vegetation and allow you the greatest chance of catching a glimpse of the Cassowary. P. LIK

Look out for cassowaries which are liable to come to the parking area in the early morning or, especially, in the evening. Remember, do not attempt to feed these big birds and stand very still while they walk around so as not to frighten them or provoke them into aggressive behaviour. Should you feel threatened by one, get behind a tree or back into your car. If you don't see a Cassowary you should at least see their trademark droppings – a colourful pile of partly digested seeds.

At the car park there is a short rainforest walk of 1.2 km with labelled trees which is the best place of all to see a variety of plant species from this unique place. There is also an excellent 350 m children's walk that follows 'cassowary' footprints to a surprise near the end of the track.

A Quandong (*Elaeocarpus angustifolius*) and gingers (*Alpinia racemigera*) fringe the view of Garner's Beach from Bicton Hill, Clump Mountain National Park, near the small town of Mission Beach. This is one of the wettest parts of the wet tropical coast where rainforest extends right to the edge of the sea.   P. CURTIS

Clump Mountain National Park

At Bingil Bay, just 2 km north of Mission Beach, is a remnant of the coastal rainforests which grew to the water's edge. The Bicton Hill Circuit track is a 4.2 km return track to a lookout. The track zig-zags up the hill until a fork in the trail provides a choice of ways to the summit. The views on a clear day past Clump Point to Dunk Island and Hinchinbrook Island make the climb worthwhile.

OTHER PLACES TO VISIT

Eubenangee Swamp National Park

Take the Bramston Beach Road from Miriwinni on the Bruce Highway and look for the turn-off to the right, 8 km from the junction. A variety of vegetation grows on these unique wetland basalt lowlands, including gallery rainforest along Alice River. As well, the poorly drained sections are dominated by the paperbark, *Melaleuca quinquinervia*.

The 1.5 km track from the parking and picnic area follows the edge of the Alice River and offers a view of the park's flora and fauna highlights. There are no other facilities here. It is possible to see Freshwater tortoises as well as the occasional Estuarine Crocodile. But

The Edmund Kennedy Memorial Trail via Lugger Bay to Kennedy Bay permits views from rocky headlands such as Tam O'Shanter Point over Bedarra Island in the clear waters of the Great Barrier Reef Marine Park. The trail passes through open eucalypt forest interspersed with rainforest elements such as Solitaire Palms (*Ptychosperma elegans*).   P. CURTIS

it is the profusion of birdlife which brings the enthusiasts, with a large variety of species that inhabit or visit the various habitats. Over 170 types of birds have been spotted here. At the lookout on the hill at the end of the track, depending on the level of cloud cover, you may get a good view of the surroundings including Mt Bartle Frere in the west.

Birds that can frequently be seen in the wetland areas include, herons, egrets, spoonbills, ibis and a variety of ducks. Each year the Black-necked Stork (Jabiru) nests in the park. With the flowering paperbarks come the honeyeaters, while the rainforest species attract the Black Butcherbird, Wompoo Pigeons and a variety of parrots.

Dunk Island National Park

Three-quarters of this island is a national park and the abundant rainforest, often with a eucalypt overstorey, has long attracted naturalists for its prolific bird-life. The writer Edmund Banfield, who made the Island his home from 1897 to 1923, popularised Dunk Island with a series of four books which received world-wide distribution. His most well-known book *Confessions of a Beachcomber,* still in print today, is a fascinating story of his life on the island, his interaction with the original inhabitants and its natural history.

Home to the stunning Ulysses Butterfly, there are 13 km of walking trails with a good long 10 km walk which takes in the 271 m summit of Mt Kootaloo. Most of the island's habitats can be traversed including the rainforested creeks, the eucalypt slopes, the mangroves and the rocky shores.

The large Dunk Island Resort provides fairly expensive accommodation. Camping is permitted at a site with all amenities near the jetty but must be booked beforehand with the QDEH at Cardwell. Well served by sea transport from Mission Beach and Wongaling Beach there are also regular air services from Cairns and Townsville.

The Kennedy Track

A recently established well-constructed walk of 7 km return starts from the boat ramp at South Mission Beach and takes you to the otherwise inaccessible Kennedy Bay. Not far south of here the explorer Edmund Kennedy began his ill-fated journey. The trail follows the beach, low cliffs and headland via Tam O'Shanter Point to the section of Hull River National Park which is on the coast. A brochure, which should be available from the start of the walk, details the features and history of the area. It is one of the best coastal walks in the Wet Tropics and has the good possibility of seeing a variety of wildlife.

The trail initially traverses coastal forests of palms, pandanus and paperbark, with views to Dunk Island. You then walk along the beach of Lugger Bay, and skirt behind a patch of mangroves through a grove of Solitaire palms *(Ptychosperma elegans)* before reaching the rainforested Tam O'Shanter Point with its views from the shelter shed at Morgans Lookout. The track then descends to Turtle Bay, past a view of a small rocky island, around more mangroves, to Kennedy Bay. Here there is a picnic area near the beach with all facilities. Swimming at any time of the year is not advised because Estuarine Crocodiles can be found in the Hull River area. The return journey simply retraces the route. Allow 3–4 hours for a relaxed walk.

CARDWELL INGHAM

CARDWELL–INGHAM

IT WAS FROM JUST NORTH OF PRESENT-DAY CARDWELL THAT Edmund Kennedy began his tragic journey to explore the far north in 1848. This expedition was to be one of the most disastrous of the time. Kennedy and his party were put ashore at Rockingham Bay to follow the Great Dividing Range to Port Albany where he would be picked up by another ship. The aim of the expedition was to find new land with potential for settlement and to establish a site for a deep water port in the north.

So badly informed about the terrain was Kennedy that the expedition of 13 people was landed with, among other supplies, one tonne of flour, 270 kg of sugar and 40 kg of tea, which was to be carried in three carts. Besides the 27 horses there were 89 sheep. The entourage spent a week traversing the littoral forests looking for a way out before having to turn south, a course which ran into mangrove wetlands.

A month later they ascended the Cardwell Range where they encountered the region's dense rainforests. They were then forced to abandon their carts and were making only a few kilometres a day, having to cut their way through the forests in mountainous terrain.

After 10 weeks the expedition was only 16 km north from their starting point on the coast, although well inland. Once the party was clear of the rainforests the going was somewhat easier, but the bad start to the journey had taken its toll on the morale and health of the travellers. And while initially the coastal Aborigines were helpful, eventually there were constant altercations with different tribes culminating in the shooting of four men by Kennedy's party.

The rest of the journey became a race to meet their midway rendezvous at Princess Charlotte Bay and when that failed, Port Albany. On the eastern slopes of the McIlwraith Ranges they again came across rainforests which proved too much for eight of the party who had to be left at a base camp while the other five pushed on.

Three more of the remaining group were left behind and Kennedy and his Aboriginal assistant Galmarra made their way to within sight of their destination before the leader was killed by a party of Aborigines. Galmarra's courage in attempting to protect Kennedy, and his arduous final leg of the journey to reach the waiting vessel, has been well documented.

Thirty-four years later came Carl Lumholtz, the much quoted observer of the Aborigines, who was also a zoologist. His main reason for trekking the rainforests of this region in 1882 was to find the rare tree kangaroo. His search for animal specimens took him to remote and seemingly inaccessible rainforests through which he travelled on foot along the watercourses. After much searching, a tree kangaroo was found by his Aboriginal travelling companions. It came to be known as *Dendrolagus lumholtzii*. Lumholtz gave a clear description of the rainforest which is equally appropriate for today.

> On first entering the scrub, the solemn quiet and solitude which reign are striking. You work your way through it by the sweat of your brow; you startle a bird, which at once disappears, and your prevailing impression is that there is no life. But if you come there in the early morning or towards evening, and sit down quietly, it is surprising to see the birds approaching gently, as if they had been called, and disappearing as noiselessly as they came.

While George Dalrymple had opened the way for a track inland from the newly-formed port of Cardwell in 1864, it was not until 1872, when the Gairloch sugar mill opened, that the region established an economic base. By the 1880s Lumholtz noted the Herbert River valley as being 'thoroughly cultivated; and a steam-plough even having been brought here'. Clearing was in full swing and he lamented that the 'field of the naturalist' was 'daily disappearing'. Although he could still see the tracks of the Cassowary, he thought the only animal not

This early engraving of two Aboriginal figures set in the forest at Dalrymple Creek appeared in Carl Lumholtz's account of his expedition.

Relief from the summer heat is had in the popular swimming holes set amongst rock benches in a riparian community dominated by Water Gums (*Tristaniopsis exiliflora*), Golden Pendas (*Xanthostemon chrysanthus*) and Weeping Bottlebrush (*Callistemon viminalis*). The view depicted here is from the Murray Falls Lookout.   R. RITCHIE

disturbed by 'the restless work of man' was the crocodile.

Cardwell, once proclaimed for its potential as a northern port, is today a small fishing and tourist town, strung out along the highway, located about half-way between Townsville and Cairns. Ingham, 55 km south, is the commercial and administrative centre for the sugar cane growing Herbert River Valley. Both towns are stepping-off points for a whole range of World Heritage sites from the towering Hinchinbrook Island located within the Great Barrier Reef Marine Park to the rainforested ranges of the Wet Tropics.

Murray Falls State Forest
Located at the foothills of the Kirrama Range, 22 km west of the highway between Tully and Cardwell. This well maintained camping area is popular because of the natural pools which have been sculptured out of the rocks and which are used as swimming holes on hot days. It is also well frequented as a stopover by travellers journeying from Cairns to Townsville. The day facilities are excellent and those who wish to stay longer are catered for with a self-registering camping area with all amenities.

The granite boulders strewn at the base of the falls create a series of smaller waterfalls which, together with the rush of water which comes over the large rocks, makes an awe-inspiring sight. This is particularly so after heavy rain when it is not the time to swim as the currents are dangerous. Also, at various times the rocks can be slippery and there have been serious accidents and deaths here, so take care. The recent construction of a boardwalk has made the visit safer.

Beginning on the opposite side of the camping area is a 1.8 km return walking trail to the viewing area at the top of the falls. A track winds up the hill through rock-strewn rainforest, to emerge abruptly into dry eucalypt country. Here the aspect, soil, and fire frequency have determined the division between the two types of forest.

The walk ends at a viewing platform which allows you to take in the views over the falls. As well, the panoramic view of the Murray Valley is heightened by the rainforested Kirrama Ranges in the distance. If you attempt this walk on a hot day you will notice the difference in temperature when you enter the cool rainforest on your return walk. For further information contact the QDPI office in Cardwell.

Edmund Kennedy National Park

Just 4 km north of Cardwell or 6 km south of the small town of Kennedy is a sign pointing east to this national park which is named after the ill-fated explorer who began his journey near here. With a variety of vegetation and abundant wildlife, this park has only three drawbacks: in the warmer months mosquitoes can be persistent, sandflies are present and Estuarine Crocodiles inhabit the creeks which flow through this area. However, this coastal habitat is rare within the Wet Tropics World Heritage Area. It is a repository of great biodiversity with the chance to see wetland, woodland and rainforest plant and animal species.

After 1 km drive from the highway ignore the turn-off to the right to the camping area (now closed) and stay on the road, passing the ranger station, until you reach the beach to get to the beginning of two walking track options. The access road is unsuitable for vehicles towing caravans.

At the end of the road is a short walk to a picnic area with tables. From here there is a choice of two easy, level walks. There is either a 5 km anti-clockwise circuit walk passing through melaluca, mangrove and woodland habitats or a 6 km return walk along coast and beach (only at low tide) to Wreck Creek. For the anti-clockwise walk take the left fork 1 km from the picnic area and return 4 km via a track with a series of boardwalks which take you across the mangrove wetlands, then to the road which leads to the picnic area. On the walk you will notice the thin red flaking bark of the Red Beech (*Dillenia*

Mangrove systems are highly productive communities which function as vital plant nurseries, play a critical role in filtering the runoff on to the reef and act as seaward buffers for terrestrial communities.   R. RITCHIE

alata) as well as paperbarks and pandanus.

If, instead, you continue on to Wreck Creek you pass through lowland littoral rainforest, adjacent to the beach, to another picnic area which marks the end of the walk. The views from the beach are impressive. On your return, when you reach the fork you either go left and along the track adjacent to the beach to your starting point back over the same route, or turn right and continue on the anti-clockwise route and eventually via the road, to return you to the start. The full walk will take less than 3 hours. For further information contact the QDEH office in Cardwell which runs occasional guided walks or the Edmund Kennedy ranger station.

Dalrymple Gap Walking Track

Last century, the pastoralist George Dalrymple followed Aboriginal pathways to gain access to his property, 'Valley of Lagoons' in the Burdekin River catchment to the west. It was used until the 1870s when a more direct route to the newly-established town of Townsville was found. Later traffic included gold seekers and mail carriers.

From a turn-off 15 km south of Cardwell, it is just 1 km to a parking area at Damper Creek which is the start of a 9 km walking track through a gap in the Cardwell Range to the carpark in Abergowrie State Forest. Allow at least 5 hours one way for the trek or

4 hours return for a walk, via an old bridge and the Gap, to Dalrymple Creek. A permit must be obtained from the QDPI office in Ingham before you begin this walk. If you don't wish to re-trace your steps you should arrange for a lift back from the carpark at the end of this walk.

A one-hour 3 km (one way) walk through open eucalypt forests with rainforest creeks and gullies follows the original track to the well-preserved stone bridge, still in place over 130 years after it was built. After passing through the gap in the range, the track, rough in places and often muddy, descends the western side of the range to meet Dalrymple Creek, a further 2 hours walking. Parts of the old road are still discernible. The choice here is to return or to follow the creek banks through rainforest to the carpark in Abergowrie State Forest (another 2 hours). Camping is not permitted at either end or along the track. Contact the QDEH Cardwell office for further information and details on occasional guided walks.

Lumholtz National Park

Wallaman Falls

Wallaman Falls is the most visited part of this park. With three-quarters of the 52 km journey from Ingham on an unsealed road, parts of it very rough, this trip is best undertaken in good weather. But don't be

Wallaman Falls are certainly one of the most spectacular landscape features of the Wet Tropics. They are formed as Stoney Creek plunges over three hundred metres down the escarpment of a deeply incised gorge to join the Herbert River and on to the sea at Ingham.   P. LIK

Trunks of trees such as this Bumpy Satinash (*Syzygium cormiflorum*) are animal highways. Having flowers and fruit emerge directly from the trunk – called 'cauliflory' – is the best way to exploit this highway to maximise chances for animal pollination and seed dispersal. R. RITCHIE

deterred, the view of the Falls from the top, a scenic drive through eucalypt forest and rainforest and the possibility of a walk to the bottom of the gorge, all make for a great day's journey. A well maintained camping area has all the facilities necessary for a pleasant overnight stop. The road is not suitable for caravans because the climb up the Seaview Range is steep and winds around tight bends in places. Drivers should exercise caution.

The lookout to the Falls is 2 km from the camping area and there are good day facilities here including toilets. From the lookout you can view Stoney Creek, spilling 70 m off the Seaview Range before it tumbles a clear fall of 305 m to a large pool at its base. At times when the creek is swollen the water disappears into a cloud of mist. For those interested in the biggest and the best, Wallaman Falls is reputed to be the largest clear drop waterfall in Australia. A 1.7 km track leads down to the base of the falls. A degree of fitness is best for the full walk down and back, since the climb back up is strenuous. However, a walk of just 300 m will afford an excellent view of the gorge. The view of the falls from the bottom is a unique experience, particularly when it becomes a torrent during the Wet Season.

Back at the camping area there is a 500 m walk to a rock pool swimming spot. Much of the surrounding forest has been logged in the past but there are several places where it is possible to stop by the road and take a short walk. Birds to be seen or heard here include whipbirds, scrubwrens, parrots and honeyeaters.

If you have any doubts about road conditions check at the QDEH office in Ingham.

OTHER PLACES TO VISIT

Broadwater State Forest Park

This popular park, part of Abergowrie State Forest and just outside the World Heritage Area, is located 47 km west of Ingham via Trebonne. The final few kms pass through pine plantations from which will come the timber of the future. The route is well signposted and mostly sealed but there is a low-level bridge which can make the road impassible at times in the Wet Season. Here you will find an excellent picnic and camping area from where two very different walks begin.

Boyd's Forest Dragon
Hypsilurus boydii

With a diet of rainforest fruits, slugs and insects this spectacular animal is kept busy scavenging for food. It is commonly seen near waterways although you have to look hard to see it because it is well camouflaged with its surroundings. As a means of protection it can puff up its yellowish throat pouch and extend its jaw in a threatening display. This common reptile is endemic to the Wet Tropics. Measuring as long as 20 cm from nose to tail, the colouring of Boyd's Forest Dragon can vary with location. Busy during the day, at night it prefers the safety of a perch high in the trees. M. PROCIV

Rainforest Walking Track

One of the last remaining patches of lowland rainforest in the Ingham area, this 1.6 km walk is highly recommended to see the great variety of trees, shrubs and vines which provide food and shelter for a whole range of animals. A walk of 200 m brings you to the massively buttressed Broadwater Fig, which is at least 200 years old. As you walk its surrounding boardwalk you get to appreciate not only its dimensions but you should also recognise its role as a home for many animals.

A 1.2 km circuit walk leads off from here and many of the plants are named for easy identification. Milky Pines, Silver Quandongs *(Elaeocarpus angustifolius)*, Black Beans *(Castanospermum australe)*, Alexandra palms and even a fan palm can be spotted. At least two Scrub Fowl mounds can be seen from this trail. These birds build a nest of dirt and vegetation to lay their eggs in, with the mound acting as an oven to incubate the eggs by natural heat. Scratchings and rakings indicate whether it is used or not. They eat insects and fruit and new leafy shoots from trees and shrubs.

The track is easy walking and all level. It winds around and comes back along Broadwater Creek where Platypuses have been seen.

Broadwater Creek Track

A second 3 km return level trail leads from the northern edge of the camping area. Following an old road, this is a good bird watching walk through open forest. After 10 mins an offshoot to the left takes you to a small lookout over the creek. About 1 km from the start there is a swimming hole in the creek and just past here are Willies Rapids.

From here the forest changes to a mixture of wet and dry sclerophyll. There is also a second swimming hole off to the left. In about half-an-hour of easy walking you come to the end of the trail which is at a bend of the creek. There is no further access from here. On one side of the creek is the rocky overflow and open sclerophyll vegetation, while on the other closed forest or rainforest clings to the high bank.

Cardwell Forest Drive

This 9 km drive starts from Cardwell and finishes on Ellerbeck Road. Passing through a variety of forest types including pine plantations, there are a number of stopping points which include scenic views, walks, picnic spots and, in season, swimming holes. A brochure is available at the commencement of the drive and includes facts and fig-

The Yellow-footed Antechinus (*Antechinus flavipes*) shown here larger than life-size, is a carnivorous marsupial which may be spotted feeding on the likes of beetles and spiders during the daytime. Breeding only annualy in July or August. the frenzied mating session results in the death of the excessively-stressed male.   M. TRENERRY

ures on the Caribbean Pine *(Pinus carribea)* forest which has been established to provide local mills with a sustainable resource. The forest service has left some natural vegetation as corridors for wildlife, water catchment and soil stability. In some Wet Seasons these places provide temporary roosting sites for flying foxes. The round trip from Cardwell is 23 km via Ellerbeck.

More interesting stops include the Cardwell Lookout with fine views over Edmund Kennedy National Park, Rockingham Bay, local countryside and out to Dunk Island. By taking a 500 m walk along the steep track from the carpark, Hinchinbrook Island and the mangrove-lined channel can be viewed. About 5 km further along, at Attie Creek, there are picnic facilities and a series of falls, cascades and pools which are the most reliable swimming spots on the Drive. A 500 m steep walking trail leads to a deep pool at the foot of a 30 m waterfall.

Picnic facilities are also provided at Dead Horse Creek, another popular swimming place, which features a narrow crevice in the bedrock through which the creek passes in a torrent after heavy rainfall. It is possible to follow the creek upstream and discover for yourself the many deep pools, waterfalls and interesting rock formations. Just 1 km further on is Scrubby Creek, again with picnic facilities, where a natural spa pool, at its best during the Wet Season, invites swimmers on a hot day.

Blencoe Falls

These falls are 81 km from Cardwell on a road that is trafficable in dry weather only. Turn left at the Kennedy store, 10 km north of Cardwell and follow the bitumen for 7 km before turning right into the partly gravelled Kirrama Road. Travel a further 29 km before turning left at the Blencoe Falls sign. From here it is 18 km to Blencoe Creek along which are several picnic spots. A walking track (approximately 20 mins each way) to the top of the falls leads from the first of these picnic places.

Beyond the picnic spots the road crosses the creek and 1 km from the bridge is the turn-off which leads for 6 km to a good lookout with views across the Falls and over the Herbert River Gorge.

Allow a full day for this journey and remember that there are no provision or fuel stops after the Kennedy store.

Goold Island National Park

Located 17 km north-east of Cardwell and just to the north of Hinchinbrook Island, this 8 km² island consists of eucalypt woodland with gullies of rainforest. The only walks are on various discreet tracks

Hinchinbrook Island has many secluded coves and wonderful tropic coast scenery. Here, at Ramsay Bay on the eastern side of the island, is the start of the east coast walk known as the Thorsborne Trail.   P. CURTIS

around the island. Well-known for its flocks of Sulphur-crested Cockatoos, their familiar cries ring out across the island. Turtles and Dugongs have been spotted as they surface from feeding on the extensive seagrass beds which exist in the shallow waters to the south and west. Access is by boat from Cardwell and a camping and picnic area on the western beach has pit toilets. A small creek at the northern end of the beach is usually dry between August and December so water must be brought over during these months. Remember, swimming is not advised in the Wet Season due to the marine stingers. For further information and camping permits contact the QDEH office at Ingham.

Hinchinbrook Island National Park

Hinchinbrook Island, Australia's largest island national park, is separated from the mainland by the shallow, narrow, mangrove-fringed Hinchinbrook Channel, scoured from sand and mud by strong tidal currents. It is possible to get boats from Cardwell and Lucinda to explore sections of Hinchinbrook and there is a world-class four-day walk that runs down the eastern side.

Rising 1121 m in the centre of the island are the jagged outcrops of Mt Bowen, largest in the chain of rugged granite crags forming the backbone of the island's southern half. To the north-west a range of lesser peaks of older volcanic rocks, similar in chemistry but finer grained than the granite, form an undulating skyline descending to the sandy beach of Hectate Point 4 km across the channel from Cardwell. A narrow 8 km long strip of sand stretches north to connect with Capes Sandwich and Richards. This is backed on the protected western side by extensive mangrove forests.

On the sheltered western slopes and in valleys, deeper soils support luxuriant growth. Between the thick mangrove carpet of the channel and the mountain tops grow dense rainforests of Milky pine, figs, Quandong, palms, vines and hundreds of other species. In places, the rainforest understorey is shaded by emergent Turpentines *(Syncarpia glomulifera)*, Pink Bloodwoods *(Eucalyptus intermedia)* and Red Mahoganies *(Eucalyptus pellita)*. These forests have many animals in common with similar habitats on the adjacent mainland, but roughly 10,000 years of separation have brought about some subtle but intriguing changes.

Nearer the exposed rocky pavements of the central mountain range, vegetation changes to scrubs, heaths and stunted eucalypts. The eastern slopes of the island support woodlands dominated by Swamp Box *(Lophostemon suaveolens)* and eucalypts, including White Mahogany *(Eucalyptus acmenoides)*. Deeply dissecting these weather-worn slopes are numerous steep valleys. Water-smoothed boulders and rock plat-

The vegetation at Cape Richards in the north of Hinchinbrook Island is a rich lowland coastal vineforest with buttressed trees and stands of the Solitaire Palm *(Ptychosperma elegans)*. A popular half-day walk begins from here.   P. CURTIS

forms make for easier walking than the tangled undergrowth and broken terrain of the slopes and ridges. The creeks, fringed by rainforest, act as corridors for fauna.

The vast mangrove forests of the channel and Missionary Bay form a continuous canopy, broken only by wide tidal creeks, which are navigable with care at high tide and provide easy access. The mangroves convert sunlight, water and mud into foliage. Fallen leaves are eaten directly, or after decomposition, by many of the inhabitants, perpetuating the cycle of nutrients in this unique marine ecosystem.

A half-day walk starts from the resort at Cape Richards in the north where a 1 km track

The Olive-backed Sunbird, a gregarious bird, is often found in the company of the Ulysses Butterfly, and is usually found in pairs. The females are the nest builders, while males appear to encourage and supervise but offer little help.

They are found throughout the Wet Tropics and can often be seen in suburban areas where they sometimes nest. They are capable of having two or three clutches a year.   RAINFOREST HABITAT

leads south of the Cape to run for 2 km down the beautiful North Shepherd Beach to the Kirkville Hills. From here you can walk for 2.2 kms around the base of the Kirkville Hills to Macushla Point camping area. About 1 km along this track it is possible to take a side trail running for 2 km to South Shepherds Beach.

Another half-day walk can begin from the Ramsay Bay boardwalk, reached by travelling a mangrove estuary from Missionary Bay. This is also the start of the four-day (three night) Thorsborne Trail. From here you can walk the 3.8 km south to the camp area by the beach at Nina Bay. After 1 km of beachwalking you cross a small ridge to reach Blacksand Beach where you pass through tall open forests of Gympie Messmate *(E. cloeziana)* to the saddle below Nina Peak. The track continues along a seasonal watercourse, skirting mangroves to the northern end of Nina Bay. Remember your boat pick-up times and return the 3.8 km to the Ramsay Bay boardwalk.

As mentioned, this is the first leg of the four-day Thorsborne Trail which traverses the eastern side of the island from Ramsay Bay via Zoe Bay to Point George in the south of island the from where you return to the mainland by boat. The QDEH have produced a

comprehensive brochure with a suggested walking schedule for the Thorsborne Trail and permits need to be obtained before setting out. They should be arranged through the Ingham office, although the permits can be picked up from either the Ingham or Cardwell offices of the QDEH. The lower sections of creeks are often dry between August and December so water must be carried, or if collected from non-flowing streams it should first be boiled.

Orpheus Island National Park

Located 20 km off the coast from Ingham south of Hinchinbrook Island, this long narrow island is particularly rich in birdlife including a variety of sea birds and the mound-building Orange-footed scrubfowl. There are several short walks with the best 3 km return crossing of the island from the resort to Picnic Bay. The best rainforest is found in the north at Iris Point. The reef fringes the island making it a popular snorkelling or diving enthusiasts' destination while beautiful sandy beaches and secluded bays are numerous. You will need to arrange your own sea or air transport because there is no ferry service. James Cook University runs a marine research station here and there is an expensive resort on the island. Camping is permitted at Yank's Jetty, South Beach and Little Pioneer Bay. Take all supplies including fresh water. For further information and permits contact the QDEH office at Ingham.

Lumholtz National Park (Mt Fox)

Located on the Seaview Range 69 km south-west of Ingham via a good road, the main attraction of this 815 m volcanic peak is the 8 km scramble to the top and back. Start the walk from just past the Mt Fox school, where a 3.5 km old roadway leads through eucalypt woodland to the 500 m track to the top. Walking around the rim of the crater, which is completely treeless, it is possible to see over the whole district as well as back into the slightly depressed centre of the cone. This is one of the youngest volcanic craters in Australia.

One of the largest of the fruit bats, the Spectacled Flying Fox (Pteropus conspicillatus) is a relatively common rainforest animal which serves a very important function in dispersing many plant species. It roosts in large camps and is the nemesis of orchardists who will shoot these animals to protect their crops.   M. PROCIV

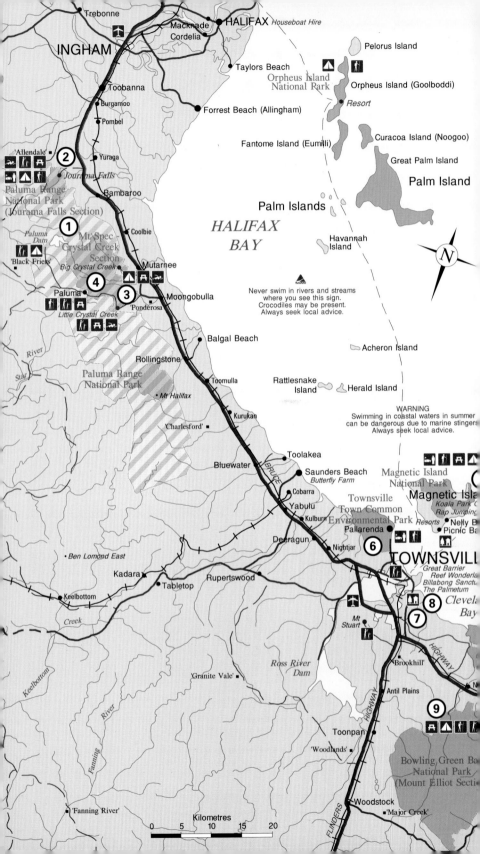

Trebonne

HALIFAX *Houseboat Hire*

Macknade
Cordelia

INGHAM

Toobanna

Burgamoo
Pombel

Taylors Beach

Orpheus Island
National Park

Pelorus Island

Orpheus Island (Goolboddi)

Resort

Forrest Beach (Allingham)

Yuraga

Fantome Island (Eumilli)

Curacoa Island (Noogoo)

Great Palm Island

Palm Island

'Allendale'

Paluma Range
National Park
(Jourama Falls Section)

Jourama Falls

Bambaroo

**HALIFAX
BAY**

Palm Islands

Havannah
Island

Coolbie

Paluma
Dam

Mt Spec
Crystal Creek
Section

Big Crystal Creek

Mutarnee

'Black Friers'

Moongobulla

Never swim in rivers and streams
where you see this sign.
Crocodiles may be present.
Always seek local advice.

Paluma

'Ponderosa'

Little Crystal Creek

Balgal Beach

Acheron Island

Rollingstone

Paluma Range
National Park

Toomulla

Rattlesnake
Island

Herald Island

Mt Halifax

Kurukan

'Charlesford'

WARNING
Swimming in coastal waters in summer
can be dangerous due to marine stingers.
Always seek local advice.

Toolakea

Bluewater

Saunders Beach
Butterfly Farm

**Magnetic Island
National Park**

Magnetic Isl

Cobarra

Yabulu

Kulburn

*Koala Park
Rap Jumping*

Nelly B

Picnic Ba

**Townsville
Town Common
Environmental Park**

Resorts

Deeragun

Pallarenda

Nightjar

TOWNSVILLE

*Great Barrier
Reef Wonderla
Billabong Sanctu
The Palmetum*

Ben Lomond East

Kadara

Tabletop

Rupertswood

BRUCE

Keelbottom

*Mt
Stuart*

**Cleve
Bay**

'Brookhill'

Creek

HIGHWAY

**Ross River
Dam**

Antil Plains

'Granite Vale'

Toonpan

'Woodlands'

Woodstock

'Major Creek'

**Bowling Green Ba
National Park
(Mount Elliot Secti**

'Fanning River'

FLINDERS

River

Star

River

Keelbottom

Fanning River

N

Kilometres

0   5   10   15   20

TOWNSVILLE

TOWNSVILLE

THE REGION WAS HOME TO THE WULGURU-KABA PEOPLE, WHO lived between the foothills and the coast, moving with the cycles of nature which allowed them to make use of abundant natural food supplies. First contact was made by Phillip King who landed his ship *Mermaid* at Cape Cleveland in 1819. The ship's botanist Allan Cunningham made a note of the Aboriginal thatched huts. Until recently, little was known about these people although their rock art remains in secluded parts of Bowling Green Bay National Park.

Founded in 1864 on the district's increasing cattle and wool-growing trade, Townsville quickly took over from Cardwell as the major northern port, despite its poor harbour facilities. Early on, pastoralists found the hardships of rearing sheep in difficult climatic conditions, combined with problems with spear grass and distance from markets, a less than profitable exercise. They also encountered fierce resistance from Aboriginal people who could see their livelihood threatened by the newcomers.

Townsville received a boost from its proximity to the newly discovered goldfields of Charters Towers in the early 1870s. As a major service centre the town grew steadily through the years with a prosperity that was derived not so much from speculation as from mercantile and government operations. In 1880 Carl Lumholtz arrived in Townsville by coastal steamer from Mackay on his way to the Herbert River district where he was planning to carry out natural history studies.

By the turn of the century, north Queensland was regarded as an exemplar of successful tropical settlement by Europeans. Talk of a separate colony for the north was common and the various primary industries had settled down enough to provide a stable workforce with steady work. As the terminus of an expanding rail network, Townsville had secured its place as the major city of north Queensland, a role it has maintained to the present day.

Paluma Range National Park

Mt Spec Section

There are two turn-offs from the Bruce Highway to the Mt Spec Section of this park, one is 61 km north of Townsville and the other is 40 km south of Ingham. From either of these turn-offs, you are on the old section of the highway and there are two roads leading off to different parts of the park. One leads to Paluma, high on the range, while

Little Crystal Creek flows through drier country from the cool upland rainforests of the Paluma Range. This stream offers pleasant swimming holes for residents of nearby Townsville and visitors alike.   P. LIK

the northerly turn-off leads to Big Crystal Creek, where there are swimming places and a camping area. Paradise Waterhole, the first of these, has a picnic and camping area with barbecues and tap water. A couple of kilometres on, a second picnic spot also has barbecues but no camping is permitted. Both places have excellent swimming holes.

The winding sealed Mt Spec Road up to Paluma was constructed in the Great Depression as an employment project. Care needs to be taken on this road but also appreciate the engineering feat and observe some of the fine stonework in the roadside and creek crossings. At Little Crystal Creek about half-way up the range, there is a car park; there are also toilets, tables and barbecues to cater for the crowds who flock here in the hot weather to cool off in the creek pools. On the way up you can also observe the mosaic of wet and dry vegetation that has resulted partly from regular fires. Fairy Falls and Maiden Hair Creek must have been named in times when the rainforest vegetation was more dominant.

Just before Paluma is the turn-off to the right to McClelland's Lookout which has good views of Halifax Bay, the Palm Islands and Crystal Creek. There is another picnic area here with abundant Brush-turkeys and a good variety of other bird life. From here there is an easy 1.5 km walking trail leading to Witt's Lookout and a further 500 m walk to the delightful Cloudy Creek which drops off steeply on its

The Red-legged Pademelon *(Thylogale stigmatica stigmatica)* shuffles along the forest floor at night feeding on leaves, berries and fern fronds. They will often also feed on the grassy verges of forests where they may be seen in the evening. When these solitary animals do get some sleep they prop up against a tree, sit on the base of their tails and drop their heads.   M. TRENERRY

path down the range. Paluma Range NP offers the opportunity to view much of the Wet Tropics birdlife and the rainforests and adjacent eucalypt woodlands are recognised as top birdwatching locations. For further information contact the QDEH office at Ingham or Paluma.

Jourama Falls Section
The turn-off to this section of the park is 91 km north of Townsville or 24 km south of Ingham. A good access road with a section of gravel stretches for 6 km to the parking, picnic and camping area. Be sure to check the depth of the causeway crossings on the access road after rain. Swimming holes abound here.

This section consists of open forest and rainforest-fringed creeks. The spurs of the Seaview Range are a catchment for the many small streams which flow towards the coast. While the higher slopes are covered with rainforest, drier open forests have developed where fires are frequent. Here, Moreton Bay Ash, Bloodwood and Poplar Gum are dominant. Look out for the fire-adapted cycads near the beginning of the walk.

Waterview Creek cascades over salmon-coloured granite at Jourama Falls. Back along the creek is vine forest surrounded by eucalypts.   P. CURTIS

Jourama Falls tumble over a series of huge boulders and massive rock faces before spilling into Waterview Creek. They are easily accessible by a 1.5 km track, beginning at the end of the road 700 m past the main camping area. Much of the walk is via the rocky path of the bed of Waterview Creek. Along the creek look out for Emerald Doves, Azure Kingfishers, Satin Flycatchers and Northern Fantails. In the creek you may see tortoises and eels.

After crossing the creek, the right fork leads to a 450 m climb up to the first lookout over the falls and the adjacent rainforest. The second lookout is a further 450 m. The track leading off to the left before the ascent to the lookouts leads to the base of the falls and the popular swimming spots. For further information contact the QDEH office at Ingham or Jourama.

OTHER PLACES TO VISIT

Paluma Township

Paluma was a tin mining centre late last century when it was known as Cloudy Creek. Within the national park and the surrounding state forests are reminders of tin mining operations which are evident today from the remains of narrow rectilinear holes in the ground. The town further evolved to cater for the timber industry which was very active in the area, particularly during World War II when the forests were harvested heavily for the war effort. At this time also the US Army had an observation post at Cloudy Clearing while the RAAF ran a small convalescent hospital in the town.

Paluma now carries on trade with the travellers who come to admire the natural values of the district. A mostly quiet little town, there are a few shops to entice the visitors as well as the people with weekenders who come here to escape the heat of Townsville. A short self-guided rainforest walk begins behind Ivy Cottage, a good spot to buy refreshments; just ask for the brochure. Opposite here, the Butterfly and Insect Museum offers an educational experience. The rainfall at Paluma averages 2850 mm per year, three times that of the surrounding district. It is the result of the clouds, cooled as they rise, dropping their moisture on the range. In fact, quite often there is a cloud mass enveloping the mountain.

Next to the Environment Centre, which is used to introduce school students to ecology, is a very short self-guided Sensory Trail aimed at increasing the visitor's appreciation of the rainforest. The idea is to take the walk with at least one other person and take turns in

Upland tropical cloud forest with feather palms such as this scene from the Paluma Range National Park has a distinctly cooler subtropical character.   PETER LIK

being blindfolded to experience the forest without sight. You will find that the senses of hearing and touching will be accentuated as you follow the directions in the pamphlet which is available at the beginning of the trail.

Bush camping is permitted at Paluma Dam, about 17 km from the township along a mostly gravel road.

Magnetic Island

Virtually a suburb of Townsville, with a permanent population of 2500, this 52 km² island offers much to see, including a national park which covers 70 per cent of the island. As much as anything the attraction here is the spectacle of the azure sky meeting the shimmering surface of the ocean to contrast with the green vegetation and buff brown granite boulders which dominate the rugged hillsides.

There are several good bushwalks which will allow you to see the flora and fauna at close-hand. The walk from Horseshoe Bay Road to The Forts is an easy one-and-a-half hour walk with a chance of seeing some descendants of the koalas which were introduced to the island about 70 years ago. The Forts, a series of observation towers and gun emplacements, are interesting structures left over from World War II.

The climb to the highest point on the island, Mt Cook (500 m), is a full-day walk which should only be attempted by those who are fit and water should be carried. At Nelly Bay a failed development site is

Townsville Town Common Conservation Park contains a variety of bird habitats and after summer rains it attracts huge flocks of wetland species.   P. CURTIS

Australian Brush-turkey
Alectura lathami

Very commonly seen at picnic spots throughout the Wet Tropics, these Megapods are well-known for the huge mounds they build to incubate their eggs. They appear to have set territories and spend their time scratching in the leaf litter for fallen seeds, fruit and small animals. Brush-turkeys get out of trouble on foot but have the ability to fly clumsily if necessary.

The incubation mounds are built and jealously guarded by males and are re-used over the years. The composting effect of the rotting leaves is closely monitored by the male and the female will lay about 20 eggs, layed one at a time every few days during the breeding season. The surviving young hatch in about seven weeks and they must burrow their way out and tend for themselves immediately.

The smaller Scrubfowl *(Megapodius reinwardt)* build even larger nests and several pairs may share a mound. Eggs are laid at the end of a two metre tunnel and reburied in the rotting mass. Scrubfowl live in coastal areas from north of Rockhampton to the tip of Cape York and in the north coast of the Northern Territory while Brush-turkeys are found from northern New South Wales to Cape York.   M. TRENERRY

a blight on the Bright Point end of the beach. A testament to the excesses of the 1980s, the project awaits environmental restoration.

Regularly served by a 20-minute ferry ride from Townsville to the jetty at Picnic Bay, there is a variety of reasonably-priced accommodation at the various settlements on the Island. It is possible to hire transport to get around including bicycles, motorbikes and the ubiquitous Mokes. Be prepared for very hot weather if you visit from October to March. For more information contact the Magnetic Island office of the QDEH.

Fungi play a major role in the break-down of dead matter and therefore in the nutrient cycling of forests. Much of a fungus consists of fine hair-like structures called 'mycelia' which penetrate dead and dying tissue. It is only when they produce fruiting bodies as shown here that they become conspicuous. M. PROCIV

Townsville Town Common Conservation Park

Located 6.5 km from the centre of Townsville, you should look out for the turn-off on the Cape Pallarenda Road past the Rowes Bay Golf Club. Hours are 6.30 am to 6.30 pm seven days. Covering 3245 ha the Common has a variety of vegetation types including mangroves, grasslands, wetlands, woodlands and vine thickets. It is renown for its waterbirds, particularly in summer when the rains turn the park into a huge wetland habitat. You may obtain a bird list from the ranger station near the entrance and you can also be directed to specially-built hides from where you should be able to spot, and perhaps photograph, a variety of species.

The Palmetum

This unique botanical garden features one family of plants, the palms (*Arecaceae*). The collection is truly representative, containing all six sub-families within the family, and nearly all the 60 species of palms which are native to Australia. The design of The Palmetum allows for excellent public viewing of the 300 planted species. In addition, the collection contains many rare and threatened species, which may help contribute to their conservation. A brochure is available which leads you on a self-guided walk through primary tropical habitats such as xerophytic, savannah, mangrove and rainforest areas. The Palmetum is open from 8.30 am to 4.30 pm Monday to Friday and is closed weekends and public holidays. Admission is free.

Billabong Sanctuary

Once a dry, barren strip of land, Billabong Sanctuary has been transformed in 10 years into an oasis for animals. Three distinctive habitats have been re-created: rainforest, eucalypt forest and wetlands. An interactive zoo, the Sanctuary is a good introduction to a variety of animals which you would have to go a long way to see in the wild. A series of talks are presented during the day to coincide with the feeding times of various animals including Koalas, Estuarine Crocodiles, Fruit Bats, Dingoes and Pythons. As well as a wetland with waterbirds there is a walk-through aviary with a number of species.

The sanctuary is also involved in the Captive Breeding Program for Cassowaries, whereby chicks are reared and released into the wild. Through their diet these big birds are responsible for dispersing more than 100 species of trees and vines, so as Cassowaries decline in numbers the rainforest ecology becomes altered.

Located 17 km south of Townsville, the Sanctuary is open 9.00 am to 5.00 pm every day of the year except Christmas Day. Admission charges are $14 for adults and $7 for children. A family pass is $36.

Alligator Creek flows through moist vineforest in Bowling Green Bay National Park at the southernmost end of the Wet Tropics biogeographic region. Found here also is Australia's southernmost microhylid or nursery frog, *Cophixalus mcdonaldi,* clearly indicating the southern limit of Wet Tropics habitats proper.   P. CURTIS

Bowling Green Bay National Park

This large coastal national park (55,300 ha) includes the majority of habitats found in the region. Dominated by Mt Elliot and Saddle Mountain, Bowling Green Bay National Park has a variety of vegetation including mangroves, coastal wetlands, open woodlands as well as tropical rainforests which are near their southern limit here. On Mt Elliot it is generally confined to areas above 600 m but it can be found following the stream beds in lower elevations. In the valleys open eucalypt forest predominates while casuarinas and callistemons border the creeks.

Look for the turn-off on the right to the camping and day-use area 26 km south of Townsville. Here you will find the start of the 6 km road to Alligator Creek day-use and camping area which has all facilities including swimming spots. It is also the starting place for two walks. This section of the park is open to day visitors between 6.30 am and 6.30 pm. Campers should notify the ranger in advance if they intend leaving the park at night.

At the campground it is common to see Agile Rock Wallabies and Rufous Bettongs feeding in the evening, while at night, Common Brushtail Possums, sugar gliders and Northern Brown Bandicoots go about their search for food. Because of the park's floristic diversity it is an excellent location to sight a variety of avifauna. Birds which are common here include herons and ibis in the wetland areas, a variety of pigeons and the Brush-turkey in the rainforests and kingfishers and cuckoo-shrikes in the open woodlands.

The Cockatoo Creek track starts from the camping area. Follow the track to Alligator Falls for 2 km to Cockatoo Creek then rock-hop upstream into the rainforest to experience the range of the park's diverse vegetation. Allow 6 hours for this 8 km return walk.

A longer 17 km return full-day walk leads to Alligator Falls with the track following the creek and, in many places, powerlines. The valley, framed by Mt Elliot and Saddle Mountain, eventually narrows. The final part of the walk is through a vine thicket and includes a scramble over rocks to reach the falls with its waterholes.

WET TROPICS FAUNA

GARRY WERREN

The Wet Tropics biogeographic region supports a fauna which is highly diverse and which contains an extraordinary degree of endemism unsurpassed by any other region in Australia. Many species are rainforest specialists because the most extensive continuous area of this vegetation type occurs here. The regional diversity is further enhanced by the existence also of many non-rainforest habitats. This is true for both the invertebrates and the vertebrates. Due to the fact that the former are so numerous and, except for the butterflies and some of the larger moths and beetles, so poorly known, attention will be focused on the great array of vertebrates which can be observed by visitors to the region. While catching a glimpse of Wet Tropics fauna can sometimes be frustratingly difficult, you would be unlucky not to see at least some wildlife on any of the walks in this book.

The Wet Tropics region contains 110 species or 36 per cent of Australia's mammal species (comprising 30 per cent of the marsupials, 58 per cent of the bats and 25 per cent of the rodents, plus both monotremes); 327 species (50 per cent) of the birds; 162 species (23 per cent) of the reptiles, at least 60 species (27 per cent) of the frogs and 64 species (37 per cent) of the freshwater fishes of the continent. Amazingly, all these are located within a region which amounts to a mere 0.1 per cent of Australia's land mass. In addition, there are also many more subspecies and races of more widespread species which are endemic to the region.

The Mammals

Endemic Wet Tropics mammals include: Atherton Antechinus (*Antechinus godmani*), two tree kangaroos *(Dendrolagus bennettii, D. lumholtzi)*, the primitive Musky Rat-kangaroo (*Hypsiprymnodon moschatus),* four ringtail possums *(Hemibelideus lumuroides, Pseudochirops archeri, Pseudocheirus cinereus, P. herbertensis)* and the Thornton Peak Mosaic-tailed Rat *(Uromys hadrourus).*There are two other endemic species found in non-rainforest habitats, both considered endangered. These are the Mahogany Glider *(Petaurus gracilis)* and the Tropical Bettong *(Bettongia tropica).*Three species of rock wallaby *(Petrogale sharmani, P. mareeba* and *P. godmani)* also occur on the western fringe of the region but extend beyond its bounds. The known Australian distributions of a further two species – the Long-tailed Pygmy Possum (*Cercartetus caudatus*) and Flute-nosed Insectivorous Bat *(Murina florium)* are confined to the Wet Tropics, but they also occur in Papua New Guinea and South-east Asia respectively. In addition to the 11 endemic mammal species, nine subspecies, many of which have major populations further to the south, are considered endemic to the region. Accordingly, those wishing to catch glimpses of around 20 of Australia's distinctive mammal taxa in the wild would need to visit the Wet Tropics.

The region also supports good populations of mammals which are not confined to the Wet Tropics but which add considerably to the wildlife diversity. Rainforest species such as the strikingly coloured Striped Possum *(Dactylopsila trivirgata)*, the Red-legged Pademelon *(Thylogale stigmatica stigmatica)*, the Prehensile-tailed Rat *(Pogonomys mollipilosus)*, the common White-tailed Rat *(Uromys caudimaculatus)* and the Spectacled Flying Fox *(Pteropus conspicillatus)* are some. Others of the woodlands, open forests and mangroves include the Short-nosed and long-nosed Bandicoots *(Isoodon macrourus* and *Perameles nasuta)*, the north-east Queensland race of the Yellow-bellied, or as known locally, the Fluffy Glider *(Petaurus australis reginae)*, Sugar Glider *(P. breviceps)* and Feather-tailed Glider *(Acrobates pygmaeus)* and the Agile Wallaby, many of the bats including the Black and Little Red Flying Foxes *(Pteropus scapulatus, P. alecto)*, the Blossom Bats *(Nyctimene robinsonii, Syconycteris australis)* as well as the Water Rat *(Hydromys chrysogaster)*.

While most animals are elusive in the wild there are many locations where visitors have a good chance of observing some of the region's distinctive mammals. The crater lakes of the Atherton Tableland are great places to see Musky Rat-kangaroos, one of the few mammals which are active by day. And since most mammals are nocturnal they are sometimes seen illuminated by moonlight or by special spotlighting equipment. There are tour operators who specialize in night visits to places where they have permits to visit. It is important to ensure that your operator uses only low wattage lights and does not encourage feeding of animals. Here Herbert River Ringtails *(Pseudocheirus herbertensis)*, Green Ringtails *(Pseudochirops archeri)*, Lemuroid Ringtails *(Hemibelideus lemuroides)* and Coppery Brushtail Possums *(Trichosurus vulpecula johnsonii)* can be observed, often at very close quarters. Several other places where visitors have a chance of seeing mammals are mentioned in the descriptions of the various walks.

Lastly, several mammals are crepuscular – meaning that they are

The Striped Possum *(Dactylopsila trivirgata)* is especially agile and able to negotiate seemingly flimsy branches. Here the act is performed with a family member on board. Feeding at night on insects found in wood, this possum uses its sharp teeth, a long tongue and an elongated fourth finger as a probe. During the day a nest in a tree hollow or amongst epiphytes serves as a sleeping place.   M. PROCIV

more active around dawn and dusk. Others which are essentially nocturnal are also more likely to be viewed at these times. A quiet observer with patience will be amply rewarded. Even without venturing far from the hotel room or campsite, even in the larger urban areas such as Cairns, Townsville, Atherton, Mossman, Port Douglas, Innisfail, Mission Beach, Tully, Cardwell or Ingham, visitors will easily see the hordes of flying foxes leaving their roosts to forage at dusk. In the early evening and around dawn, Agile Wallabies can be seen grazing on open grassy verges about such places.

The Birds

Thirteen bird species are restricted entirely to the Wet Tropics region. Like the endemic mammals, most (nine species) are confined to the upland rainforests, while the remainder are relatively widespread throughout. All have close relatives in Papua New Guinea. The Grey-headed Robin *(Poecilodryas albispecularis),* is an inquisitive and easily observed bird of the wet tropical uplands. The Golden Bowerbird *(Prionodura newtoniana)* and Australian Fern-wren *(Crateroscelis gutteralis)* are sole representatives of the maypole-building bowerbirds and mouse-warbler groups, respectively, which are otherwise entirely restricted to the New Guinean mountain forests. The Tooth-billed Bowerbird *(Scenopoeetes dentirostris)* is closely related to the Green Catbird *(Ailuroedes crassirostris)* which is also found patchily along the east coast of Australia, with the spotted subspecies *(A. c. maculosus)* confined to the Wet Tropics.

There are three species of birds of paradise in Australia with Victoria's Riflebird *(Ptiloris victoriae)* endemic to this region. Two species of shrike-thrush co-occur in Australia and its northernmost neighbour, with a third, Bower's Shrike-thrush *(Colluricincla boweri)* a Wet Tropics endemic. Similarly, three species of monarch flycatchers are found in north-eastern Australia, one of which, the Pied Monarch *(Arses kaupi)*, is exclusive to the Wet Tropics. The two endemic honeyeaters, the Bridled Honeyeater *(Lichenostomus frenatus)* and Macleay's Honeyeater *(Xanthotis macleayana)* are both related to New Guinean species, as is the Atherton Scrubwren *(Sericornis keri)* and Mountain Thornbill *(Acanthiza katherina)*. Lastly, the exclusively Australian species of two groups shared by Australia and Papua New Guinea, are Wet Tropics endemics. These are the Chowchilla *(Orthonyx spaldingii)* and Lesser Sooty Owl *(Tyto multipunctata)*. Each has sister species *(O. temmincki* and *T. tenebricosa)* which occur in the rainforests of south-eastern Australia and thousands of kilometres away in New Guinea.

A further 11 bird species are represented here by more or less distinctive Wet Tropics endemic subspecies. Among these are the brightly coloured Australian King Parrot *(Alisteris scapularis minor)* and the red-crowned Double-eyed Fig Parrot *(Psittaculirostris diopthalma macleayi),* a smaller form where the males have a more violet sheen of the Satin Bowerbird *(Ptilinorhynchus violaceus minor)* and the dark subspecies of the familiar Grey Fantail *(Rhipidura fuliginosa frerei).*

Because half of the species of Australian birds occur within the region, the Wet Tropics is a mecca for birdwatchers. Keen birdwatchers come prepared with binoculars and a good guide book. They also usually have a good knowledge of bird calls because quite often birds are more heard than seen. The more serious among them can marvel at the intricacies of identifying the many species of wader which can be closely observed from the Esplanade in the middle of Cairns, which is a city also enlivened by the shrill whistles of large flocks of lorikeets which roost in the many street trees at dusk. Meanwhile the keen 'twitchers' visit the upland forests to cross off the endemics on their checklist.

Many birds, for instance the ubiquitous Brush-Turkeys, can be seen at several of the day-use areas. Others may wish to take time to search out the most imposing of the region's birds, the Southern Cassowary *(Casuarius casuarius johnsonii)* with its large horny cask and vivid red and blue wattle. While this bird may be occasionally encountered in places such as the Blue Arrow Walk within Mt Whitfield Environment Park right in the middle of Cairns City, a more likely spot to catch a glimpse of this large flightless fruit-eater is at Licuala State Forest Park near Mission Beach.

The Reptiles

With just under one-quarter of Australia's total species, the region has a large and diverse reptile fauna. Over 30 rainforest-dependent species occur in the area. Many of these are cryptic litter skinks, some of which are restricted totally to the summit zones of the higher peaks and identifiable only by visitors with specialist interests, while others include the attractively primeval Boyd's Forest Dragon *(Hypsilurus boydii)* which can often be seen in the day time. The bizarre Chameleon or Carrot-tailed Gecko and the giant endemic Leaf-tailed Gecko *(Saltuarius cornutus)* are found throughout rainforests of the region, with the latter more common in the uplands. Also restricted to the Wet Tropics are a species of gecko *(Nactus galgajuga)* and skink *(Carlia scirtetus)* which are entirely confined to the black granite boulder jumbles of the Black Trevethan Range south of Cooktown, a rock skink *(Ctenotus terrareginae)* of coastal sclerophyll woodlands of Hinchinbrook Island and the nearby mainland, the pygopid *Delma mitella* of the eastern Atherton Tableland and a newly described elapid snake, *Cacophis churchilli*, which inhabits the drier open forests of Cairns' northern beaches and the MacAlister Range south of Port Douglas.

The largest of all the reptiles is the Estuarine or Saltwater Crocodile *(Crocodylus porosus)*. This huge saurian inhabits most of the Wet Tropics river systems and is commonly sighted from the safety of a boat or occasionally from the ferry, basking along the Daintree River or even sometimes in the lugubrious waters of Eubenangee Swamp. Its smaller cousin, the Freshwater Crocodile or 'Freshie' *(C. johnstonii)* can also be observed on the western margin of the region where it inhabits the westerly-flowing streams.

Another imposing reptile which is often observed in the rainforests of the Wet Tropics is the largest of all Australian snakes, the Amethystine or Scrub Python *(Morelia amethystina)* which can reach lengths of more than five metres. This and other non-venomous pythons such as the Carpet Snake *(Morelia spilota)* and Spotted Python *(Liasis maculosus)* can often be seen in the vicinity of many of the fruit bat colonies where they are usually assured of a meal of tasty young flying fox.

Snakes to be aware of, and carefully avoided, are more likely to be in disturbed areas such as canefields and clearings where there are piles of debris rather than in the forest. These include the Eastern Taipan *(Oxyuranus scutellatus)* and the Common Brown Snake *(Pseudonaja textilis)*.

The Frogs

By definition, the *Wet* Tropics, at the right time of the year, is a great place to see a large variety of frog species, that is if one can pick them out from the omnipresent introduced Cane Toad *(Bufo marinus)*. The region boasts the greatest number of rainforest-dependent endemic frog species in Australia with 23 of the 26 such species found nowhere

One of Australia's largest frogs, reaching over 15 cm in length, the Giant or White-lipped Treefrog *(Litoria infrafrenata)* is commonly found on the wet tropical lowlands. It is found throughout a range of habitats from paperbark-pandanus swamps, palm swamps and rainforests to suburban gardens. They can range in colour from dull olive-green to bright apple-green dorsally with white bellies. Breeding males call females with a harsh 'crunk, a crunk, a crunk'. Several of them can produce a sound like factory machinery. When attacked by a Black Butcherbird or disturbed by an inquisitive person, they utter a bleating painful wail.   M. PROCIV

else. The open sclerophyll country also supports a good range of species. Frogs are obviously best observed in wet places.

The 'southern frog' group, Myobatrachidae, while better represented within the subtropical rainforests of the Border Ranges, have three counterparts in the Wet Tropics. Two of these, the Sharp-snouted Torrent or Day Frog *(Taudactylus acutirostris)* and the Northern Tinker Frog *(T. rheophilus)* are among seven of the region's frog species which have all but disappeared over the past four years. Their fate is a cause of great concern and significant effort is being expended to attempt to determine the reason for these mysterious disappearances. The third species, the spectacular Northern Barred Frog *(Mixophyes schevilli)*, more frequently seen as large (to 13 cm) tadpoles or heard as it calls its loud sonorous 'waarks', still occurs in good numbers.

Tree frogs, the Hylidae, are widely distributed throughout the region. Five of these have been afflicted by the same sharp population crashes mentioned above and two are unlikely to be encountered by visitors at all. These include the Armoured Mist-Frog *(Litoria lorica)* and Mountain Mist Frog *(L. nyakalensis)*. The remaining three now occur in greatly reduced populations in the lowlands having been wiped out from their upland strongholds. These are the Torrent Tree Frog or Waterfall Frog *(L. nannotis)*, Common Mist Frog *(L. rheocola)* and Australian Lace-lid *(Nyctimystes dayi)*. Other tree frogs remain in good numbers and are amongst the commonest of all of the region's vertebrates. The most strikingly coloured of these include the Eastern Dwarf Green Tree Frog *(L. fallax)*, Dainty Tree Frog *(L. gracilenta)*, Giant or White-lipped Tree Frog *(L. infrafrenata)* and, the most colourful of all, the Orange-thighed Tree Frog *(L. xanthomera)*.

A very distinctive group of frogs found no further south in Australia than the Wet Tropics region are the tiny litter frogs or Microhylids. With at least 13 of Australia's current total of 18 described species, this is the most diverse of all regions for this group which has no free-swimming tadpole stage but froglets hatch directly from eggs laid in moist soil or leaf litter under fallen debris on the rainforest floor. Many of these (eg, the Carbine Nursery Frog, *Cophixalis monticola*, Bellenden Ker Nursery Frog, *C. neglectus* and Windsor Buzzing Nursery Frog, *C. bombiens)* have very restricted distributions, while others such as the Ornate Nursery Frog *(C. ornatus)* are more widespread. The Whistle Frogs or Chirpers *(Sphenophryne* spp.) are also moderately widespread within different sections of the region and lend a most distinctive charm to the forest sound-scape on rainy nights. As with all of this group, these are more likely to be heard than seen. Lastly, the sole Australian representative of the 'true frog' group, the Ranidae, also occurs here. This is the Australian Bull Frog (*Rana daemeli*). Its chuckling call is frequently part of the evensong around rainforest streams.

The Freshwater Fishes

The region supports a large number of freshwater fish species although there are few which are endemic or entirely restricted to the region. The fishes are found in lakes and streams and other waterways where they are best observed in shallow water. Of the 64 species, only a handful are regarded as endemics. These comprise the Roman-nosed Goby *(Awous crassilabrus)*, the Cairns Rainbowfish (*Cairnsichthys rhombosomoides*) and the Lake Eacham Rainbowfish (*Melanotaenia eachamensis*), the latter which is now extinct from its Type Locality. In addition, a further two undescribed species, the Mulgrave Goby *(Glossogobius* sp. nov.) and a thick-lipped grunter *(Scortum* sp. nov.) are also assumed to be endemic.

Characteristic fish assemblages which visitors can expect to encounter can be considered in relation to three different sections of aquatic habitat:

• The lower reaches of easterly flowing streams such as the Lower Mulgrave and Barron rivers and creeks such as Emmagen and Banyan typically have a rich fish fauna which represents a mixture of freshwater and estuarine species. Rainbowfish and Pacific Blue-eyes *(Pseudomugil signifer)* as well as species of gudgeon *(Eleotridae),* glassfish or perchlets *(Ambassidae),* Jungle Perch *(Kuhlia rupestris),* as well as the estuarine or sea perch (Lutjanidae) and mullet (Mugilidae), inhabit such waterways.

• The middle stream reaches lack the estuarine components. These are typified by rainbowfish, Jungle Perch, catfish (Plotosidae), gudgeons, freshwater bream or grunter (Theraponidae) together with species such as the Bullrout *(Notesthes robusta)* and Roman-nosed Goby.

• Within the upper reaches and the tableland streams, rainbowfish dominate a less species-rich assemblage along with the occasional catfish and the Trout Gudgeon (*Mogurnda adspersa*). The headwater sections at high altitudes are frequently without fish. Tadpoles and aquatic invertebrates such as the crayfish *(Euastacus* spp., *Cherax* spp.) inhabit these waters.

Wet Tropics Endemic Mammals

Atherton Antechinus
Antechinus godmani

Only up to about 16 cm long, this rat-sized nocturnal marsupial forages on the forest floor, feeding on insects. Males are active during the day in the breeding season between June and July and soon after a frenzied mating session they die. The females give birth in August to up to six young and after five weeks attached to the teats they are put in the nest.

These small mammals are confined to cool, wet rainforests above 600 m. They have been spotted from the Lamb Range in the north down to the Cardwell Range.

Long-tailed Pigmy-possum
Cereatetus caudatus

This 10 cm long marsupial usually feeds alone at night on the nectar and pollen of rainforest trees as well as on insects. Living in a spherical nest of leaves with as many as five others it makes good use of its prehensile tail to climb from branch to branch. Females may have up to three or four young.

In cold weather this pigmy-possum is able to retreat to its nest and attain a state of torpor, or lowered body temperature, to match its surroundings. It is found from the Daintree to Paluma.

Bennetts Tree-kangaroo
Dendrolagus bennettianus

About the size of a wallaby this tree-climbing kangaroo can measure up to 65 cm. With limbs like a possum it can climb with all four legs and spends much of its time in the canopy. When on the ground it can both walk and hop.

With a diet of leaves and fruit this mammal is confined to the north of the Wet Tropics at Mt Windsor Tableland, Thornton Peak and Mt Finnigan.

Lumholtz's Tree-kangaroo
Dendrolagus lumholtzi

Looking similar to Bennett's tree-kangaroo, and with a similar diet, this nocturnal mammal lives in the canopy, often by itself, but sometimes in a family or feeding group.

Its long tail is used for balance in the tree-tops and as an aid in descending trees.

Living in the upland rainforests, it has been found from Mt Carbine Tableland in the north to the Cardwell Range with extensive sitings in the Atherton Tableland.

Musky Rat-kangaroo
Hypsiprymnodon moschatus

About the size of a bandicoot, this small member of the kangaroo family is commonly seen scratching around the forest floor by day as it looks for fruits and hunts for insects. As a primitive macropod this animal is most likely a link between arboreal possums and kangaroos, although it spends all its time on the ground. At night it sleeps in a leaf nest, often at the base of a buttressed tree. The female produces two young between November and July.

The Musky Rat-kangaroo can be seen in both lowland and upland rainforests throughout the Wet Tropics.

Lemuroid Ringtail Possum
Hemibelideus lemuroides

Found mostly in the upper canopy, this nocturnal possum shelters in a tree hollow during the day and at night leaps noisily from branch to branch in search of its diet of leaves. Between August and November a single young is produced from a pouch and hitches a ride on its mother's back. Unlike other possums, these ones are often found in family or feeding groups. The Lemuroid Ringtail is found in cool, wet rainforests above 550 m from Mt Carbine Tableland to Cardwell Range.

Thornton Peak Melomys
Melomys hadrourus

With only nine specimens collected, little is known about this rodent, the largest member of its genus. Looking similar to a White-tailed Rat, the Thornton Peak Melomys has smaller hindfeet, a smaller head and a stout tail. To date it has been found on the Mt Carbine Tableland and Thornton Peak.

Green Ringtail Possum
Pseudochirops archeri

The black, white and yellow bands of hairs on the back of this appealing animal combine to give it a greenish tinge. Usually a loner, feeding on the rainforest leaves at night, it is sometimes active during the day. When it sleeps it curls up in a tight ball on a branch rather than living in a den like most other possums. The single young hitches a ride on its mother's back and remains with her for longer than other ringtails.

The most widely distributed of the four endemic ringtail possums, it is found throughout the Wet Tropics at altitudes above 300 m.

Herbert River Ringtail Possum
Pseudocheirus herbertensis

Strictly nocturnal, this possum emerges from its tree hollow or leaf nest to feed on leaves and the occasional rainforest fruit. Two young, pale brown in colour, are produced and they only spend a short time on their mother's back before being left in a nest where they are fed. By the time they are one year old they have attained the striking black back with white underbelly of their parents.

The Herbert River Ringtail Possum is found in cool, wet rainforests above 400 m from the Lamb Range on the Atherton Tableland to the Seaview Range.

Daintree River Ringtail Possum
Pseudocheirus cinereus
Only recently was this species been separated from the Herbert River Ringtail Possum which is of similar size and which has similar habits. The most obvious difference is its brownish-grey colouring with a dark stripe on its forehead. It is found above 450 m from north of Thornton Peak to Mt Lewis on the Carbine Tableland.

Tube-nosed Insectivorous Bat
Murina florium

This tiny bat measuring only 5 cm in length has adapted to the wet forests by wrapping its wings around its body to keep it dry. Feeding on insects and nectar, it maintains contact with others of its type by a distinctive call. This extremely rare species has only been found at Mt Baldy and Mt Hypipamee NP on the Atherton Tableland.

Wet Tropics Endemic Birds

Mountain Thornbill
Acanthiza katherina

This bird, an adult male, has olive-green feathers on its back and a cream breast and feeds in flocks on the foliage of the upper canopy. Recognised by its soft, pleasant warble it is commonly found in the cool, wet rainforests above 600 m from Mt Finnigan to Paluma. From June these birds build a dome-shaped nest with a side entrance in the middle levels of the forest.

C. & D. FRITH/FRITHFOTO

Tooth-billed Bowerbird
Scenopoeetes dentirostris

This bird is only found in the cool, wet forests above 600 m ranges throughout the Wet Tropics where it is relatively common. During the breeding season from August to December the adult male will sing a medley of different songs including whistles and chuckling noises. It also attracts females by clearing a patch on the forest floor and decorating it with green leaves. The female lays two creamy eggs in a well-hidden nest several metres above the ground. These birds eat fruit and insects from the canopy as well as feeding on the foliage.

Pied Monarch
Arses kaupi

Another endemic to the lowland and upland rainforests of the area, the Pied Monarch is also found in the tall open forests. These small black and white birds, usually seen in pairs, feed busily up and down tree trunks attempting to get a feed of insects from under the bark. Their lichen-decorated small nest usually hangs between two vines.

Bowers Shrike-thrush
Colluricincla boweri

This bird usually inhabits the cool, wet rainforests above 600 m although it is known to move to lower elevations in winter. Recognised by their grey back and ochre-coloured breasts these birds forage at all levels of the rainforest.

Breeding in October, the female lays its eggs in a nest consisting of a cup of leaves and bark several metres above the ground.

Australian Fernwren
Crateroscelis gutturalis

These small birds are commonly found in the rainforests above 600 m where they hop about scratching through the damp forest-floor litter in search of insects. Although they are common they are shy and only observed by those with time and patience. Their calls include a scolding chattering sound and a high-pitched whistle. Eggs are laid between August and February and the nest, dome-shaped with a side entrance, can be found by a creek bank or in a cave.

C. & D. FRITH/FRITHFOTO

Chowchilla
Orthonyx spaldingii

This common bird is only found in this area and can live in both highland and lowland rainforests although they are more common in the latter location. The loud, dis-

tinctive 'chow-chowchilla' call of this bird is heard in the forest at dawn and dusk. Although both sexes have distinctive white circles around their eyes and dusky olive backs, the female, shown here, is distinguished by her rufous breast compared to the male's white one.

Chowchilla's blend in with their surroundings as they scratch around the forest floor in a feeding frenzy looking for insects. While they do not fly well they can run very quickly. Their nests are dome-shaped and built near the ground.

Grey-headed Robin
Poecilodryas albispecularis

This bird is only found in the cool, wet forests above 400 m ranges throughout the Wet Tropics where it is relatively common. Recognised by the distinctive tortoise-shell pattern of its plumage, it is often spotted on the edges of tracks and clearings as it dives for insects on the ground.

Bridled Honeyeater
Lichenostomus frenatus

Endemic of the highlands above 600m this is another bird which will come to the lowlands in winter. Easily recognised by their black and yellow facial pattern and the white spot behind the eye, these birds often wrestle each other in a display of apparent aggression. They can be observed in flocks as they feed off the nectar of flowering trees.

Golden Bowerbird
Prionodura newtoniana

Restricted to cool, wet rainforests above 800 m, this bird is the smallest of bowerbirds. Their diet consists mostly of fruit. The golden colours belong to the mature male, shown here, who is responsible for a spectacular bower consisting of towers of sticks, up to 2.5 metres high, placed around two small trees with a decorated branch on which to display in between. Usually attracting a number of olive-brown and ash-grey females, the male will mate with many females who then return to nests where they rear the young.

Atherton Scrubwren
Sericornis keri

Endemic to the northern part of the Wet Tropics this bird is found commonly in rainforest above 600 m. These small brown birds live in pairs and nest in dense undergrowth, and are likely to live in the one place.

Victoria's Riflebird
Ptiloris victoriae

Widely distributed throughout the Wet Tropics, the male species of this satin-black bird of paradise is renown for its spectacular courting display. Arching his rounded wings over his head and bringing his tail up at the back the male then throws his head back and sways to display its blue-green front feathers. All this to the accompaniment of a loud call which attracts many brown–grey females who are able to compare the males' display before mating with the one of their choice. Females, like the one shown here, are responsible for building the nest, hatching the eggs and rearing the young.

These birds flit around the trunks of trees, looking under bark for insects. They also use their bills to peel fruit and small flocks of these birds can dominate feeding of fruit-bearing trees by chasing other birds away.

Lesser Sooty Owl
Tyto multipunctata

While only ocurring in the Wet Tropics this nocturnal carnivore is found at a variety of elevations. Able to hunt in the forest, and getting a meal from both the tree-tops and the forest floor, its diet consists of insects, other birds and even possums. Home territory is guarded throughout the year and the nest site is mostly a convenient hollow of a tree. Courtship is a frenetic duet around the nest where the female will eventually incubate the young, relying on the male to keep up a supply of food.

C. & D. FRITH/FRITHFOTO

Macleay's Honeyeater
Xanthotis macleayana

This common bird is extensively distributed throughout the area. A shy, silent bird it is difficult to spot as it spends its time feeding, alone or in pairs, in the middle and upper parts of the forest where it searches out nectar. It also looks for insects and spiders.

FURTHER READING

Banfield, E.J., *The Confessions of a Beachcomber*, Brisbane, 1994.

Beale, E., *Kennedy of Cape York*, Adelaide, 1970.

Bolton, G.C., *A Thousand Miles Away, A History of North Queensland to 1920*, Canberra, 1963.

Breedon, S. and Cooper, W., *Visions of a Rainforest: A year in Australia's tropical rainforest*, Sydney, 1992.

Buvids, E. & Kendell, J., *Earth First! The Struggle to Save Australia's Rainforests*, Sydney, 1987.

Cooper, W. & Cooper, W.T., *Fruits of the Rainforest*, Sydney, 1994.

Erbacher, J. & S., *Survival in the Rainforest*, Sydney, 1991.

Figgis, P., *Rainforests of Australia*, Sydney, 1985.

Francis, W.D., *Australian Rainforest Trees*, Canberra, 1985.

Frith, C. & D., *Australian Tropical Reptiles and Frogs*, Malanda, 1991.

Frith, C. & D., *Australian Tropical Birds*, Paluma, 1985.

Frith, C. & D., *Australia's Wet Tropics Rainforest Life*, Malanda, 1992

Harmon-Price, P., *Shades of Green: Exploring Queensland's Rainforests*, Brisbane, 1993.

Idriess, Ion, *Men of the Jungle*, Sydney, 1943.

Keto, A & Scott, K., *Tropical Rainforests of North Queensland: Their Conservation Significance*, Canberra, 1986.

Loos, N., *Invasion and Resistance*, Canberra, 1982.

Low, Tim, *Wild Food Plants of Australia*, Sydney, 1991.

Lumholtz, C., *Among Cannibals*, London, 1889 (Reprinted ANU, Canberra 1980).

Nix, H.A. and Switzer, M.A, *Rainforest Animals: Atlas of Vertebrates Endemic to Australia's Wet Tropics*, Canberra, 1991.

Pearson, S. & A., *Rainforest Plants of Eastern Australia*, Sydney, 1992.

Pedley, H. (ed), *Aboriginal Life in the Rainforest*, Cairns, 1992.

Ritchie, R., *Seeing the Rainforests in 19th-Century Australia*, Sydney, 1989.

Rowan, E., *A Flower Hunter in Queensland and New Zealand*, London, 1898.

Russell, R., *Daintree: Where Rainforest Meets the Reef*, Malanda, 1994.

Savage, Paul, *Christie Palmerston Explorer*, Townsville, 1992.

Thomas, T., *50 Walks in North Queensland*, Melbourne, 1994.

Toohey, E., *Kie Daudai: Notes and sketches from Cape York*, Ravenshoe, 1994.

Wheeler, T. & Armstrong, M., *Islands of Australia's Great Barrier Reef*, Melbourne, 1994.

Webb, L.J. and Kikkawa, J., *Australian Tropical Rainforests: Science, Values, Meaning*, Melbourne, 1990

INDEX

Abergowrie State Forest, 132,133,135
Alexandra Lookout, 60
Alexandra Palms, 45,121, 136
Alice River, 123
Alligator Creek, 156
Angiosperms, 21,22,45,46
Atherton, 28,88,92,97,99
Atherton Tableland, 29,30, 32,33,34,36,37,68,84,85, 89,90,96,97,98,112
Babinda, 108,113,114
Barron Falls Lookout, 73,75
Barron Falls Railway Station, 75
Barron Falls Road, 73
Barron Gorge, 68,75
Barron Gorge National Park, 70,72
Barron Gorge Road, 73,76
Barron River, 68,69,71, 73,76,79,80,84
Bennett's Tree-kangaroo, 62
Bicton Hill, 123
Big Crystal Creek, 146
Big-spotted Catbird, 97
Billabong Sanctuary, 155
Bingil Bay, 108
Black Mountain, 54
Black Mountain NP, 64
Black Walnut, 90
Blencoe Falls, 138
Bloomfield River, 27,34, 39,54,55,84
Bloomfield Road, 38
Blue Arrow Trail, 79
Boulders, The, 108,110, 111,112,114
Bowling Green Bay NP, 146,156
Boyd's Forest Dragon, 62, 86,97,135
Broadwater Fig, 136
Broadwater State Forest Park, 135
Broken Nose, 116,117

Brown Salwood Wattle 73,95
Bruce Highway, 113, 120,123,146
Brush-tailed Bettong, 24
Brush-turkey, 26,73,86,90, 110,113,147,156
Bumpy Satinash, 77,86,90, 97,134
Butterfly Sanctuary, 72
Cairns, 36,55,59,68,70,72, 73,75,76,77,78,79,80, 108,125,130
Callistemon, 21
Cape Cleveland, 146
Cape Kimberley, 61
Cape Grafton, 54
Cape Richards, 140,141
Cape Sandwich, 140
Cape Tribulation, 31,38, 49,54,59,60,61,62
Cape York Peninsula, 31, 91
Carbine Tableland, 56,48
Cardwell, 31,125,126,130, 131,132,136,138,139,146
Cardwell Forest Drive, 136
Cardwell Range, 31,34,50, 128,132
Cassowary, Southern, 24, 73,111,120,155
Cedar Bay NP, 64
Cedar Creek, 28
Cedar Falls, 117
Centenary Lakes, 79
Charters Towers, 146
China Camp, 34
Cloudy Creek, 147,150
Clump Mountain NP, 123
Clump Point, 123
Cockatoo Creek, 156
Cooktown, 32,54
Cooper Creek, 120
Cooper Point, 120
Copperlode Dam, 77,78
Cow Bay, 61
Cowie Beach, 62
Crater Lakes NP, 86,92

Crawfords Lookout, 117
Crystal Cascades, 77,78
Daintree, 54,55,59,122
Daintree Environment Centre, 65
Daintree River, 32,54,56, 59,60,61,65
Dalrymple, George, 31, 129,132
Dalrymple Creek, 129,133
Damper Creek, 132
Danbulla Forest Drive, 92, 96,97
Devils Pool Walk, 114
Dinner Creek, 88,89
Dinner Falls, 89
Djabuganydji, 68
Dodd, F., 70
Douglas Creek, 118,119
Dunk Island, 107,123,124, 125,138
Eastern Whipbirds, 87
Edmund Kennedy Memorial Trail, 124
Edmund Kennedy NP, 131,138
Elinjaa Falls, 100,102
Ella Bay, 120
Ella Bay NP, 119
Ellerbeck Road, 136
Emerald End, 84
Emmagen Creek, 64
Endeavour River, 31
Estaurine Crocodile, 60, 62,68,123,125,131,155
Eucalyptus, 21,22
Fan Palm, 49,121
Fitzroy Island, 80
Flecker Botanic Gdns, 79
Flying Fish Point, 119
Flying foxes, 73
Freshwater Creek, 77
Galmarra, 27,128
Garner's Beach, 123
Gillies Highway, 85,92,97, 108,112
Gold Hill, 34
Golden Bowerbird, 62,88